Whisky with dinner

Bernard Poirier

GSPH

Published by

GSPH GENERAL STORE
PUBLISHING HOUSE INC.

1 Main Street, Burnstown, Ontario, Canada K0J 1G0
Telephone (613)432-7697   Fax (613)432-7184

ISBN 0-919431-50-X

Printed and bound in Canada.

Designedby Marlene McRoberts and Leanne Enright

General Store Publishing House Inc. gratefully acknowledges the
assistance of the Ontario Arts Council.

Canadian Cataloguing in Publication Data

Poirer, Bernard E., 1929-
    Whisky with dinner

ISSBN 0-919431-50-X

    1. Whiskey — Scotland. I. Title.
TP605.P64 1991   641.2'52'09411   C91-090479-0

First Printing November 1991

This book is dedicated
to all those who try
to make this world
a better place in which to live
- without thought of personal gain.

Acknowledgements

No book is complete without a word of thanks to all those behind the scenes who contribute to the end result. Mine is no exception. It would probably start with my friend Fergus who introduced me to malt Scotch whisky so very many years ago. Having been suitably impressed with the malt Scotch, I asked Fergus if he would be kind enough to pour some of the best upon my grave as I made my way to the great distillery in the sky. "To be sure, laddie," he agreed, then with a twinkle in his eye, added softly, "but y' wouldn't be mindin' if I filtered it through my bladder first, would y'?"

Constant encouragement came from my fellow members of An Quaich, particularly David Matthew, who officiated at the first reading. Mrs. Ann and Dr. James Withey provided technical advice and protected me from error in my ways. My wife, Carmen, as constant consultant, showed extreme patience, and so did I.

More names will simply get me into trouble and I have enough as it is.

B. E. P.

CONTENTS

INTRODUCTION

**No longer drink only water but use a little wine for the
sake of your stomach and your frequent ailments.**
(I Tim. 5:23)

What better source for sound, sage advice than the Holy Book
itself? Were it not for the time at which the statement was made,
many years before malt Scotch whisky was ever filtered through
mortal coils, Timothy would not be so easily forgiven for overlook-
ing the amber fluid in favour of the fruit of the grape. Nevertheless
his admonishment to "...use a little" is sound and holds as much
today as it did then.

For many, many years now, wines and beers have been the
traditional companion of food on the dinner table. Wines in
particular are considered as giving the added touch of elegance,
that extra element that makes any meal an occasion.

Books, nay, encyclopaedias have been written about the
selection of wines to accompany specific hors d'oeuvres, entrées
or desserts. One must concede, however, that beer rates a distant
second in this respect, not necessarily to the wide variety of wines
and the oepiminic science, but certainly to the prestige and
affluence associated with the best wines.

Very little has been written in the same vein about malt Scotch
whisky and part of the fault can be laid to rest on the Scots
themselves, who have been very much unaware of their own
national drink. This is really most unfortunate because malt Scotch
whisky is probably one of the most salubrious spirits in existence
and is particularly good with food - a most happy discovery which
was made quite accidentally, as are most finds and which, must
be shared with others. Thus the reason for this book. Another

reason why malt Scotch whisky is relatively unknown is its still-recent discovery as a very "in" drink by the trend setters. But all too often "in" things are little else than fads that quickly fade away. However, in this instance, there is every indication that such is not the case.

Scotch whisky generally has long been considered a strong spirit, lacking couth and associated with the rough and tumble rowdy males of the species. The smell alone suggests it is the antithesis of gentility and certainly not a drink for the ladies, at least not the ones worthy of that designation.

But now there is a growing recognition of malt Scotch whisky for what it is, indeed, what it has been from the beginning: uisge beatha, a veritable water of life.

Although malt Scotch whisky is presently considered a drink of occasion, a sipping spirit; it is an extremely versatile liquor which can compete quite well with any wine at mealtime, any liqueur as a pousse-café and any aperitif before meals; a somniferous element that far surpasses patent pills on the market, and generally a bloody good drink.

Introducing the reader to this amber liquid is a labour of love. Being able to share my experience and confident of the outcome is recompense in itself. We are not dealing here with any ordinary run-of-the-mill blended Scotch whisky, but rather the basis of all Scotch whiskies, the original water of life - malt Scotch whisky. After the introduction, the reader will no doubt be both surprised and pleased that this liquor is not only an exceptional drink, but that there is a brand "for all seasons." This will surely be followed by astonishment at how well and to what extent the proper malt Scotch whisky can enhance virtually any meal.

Unfortunately, translating the above from theory to practice might prove somewhat difficult at this time unless malt Scotch whisky is readily available in your area. In most parts of Canada it is not, and this is what individuals and societies such as **An Quaich** are trying to change. Indeed, the situation could be amended quite easily were it not for our peculiar liquor laws, red tape, government's thirst for taxes and a very corpulent industry. For the present time then, unless the reader is somewhat resourceful, it will be necessary to just dream about it.

The author's personal collection.

In order to be able to live the contents of this book, and experience the full range of food and spirits combinations, a malt Scotch equivalent of a well-stocked wine cellar would be necessary, either in the restaurant or in the home. Unfortunately, this is not feasible at the present time. What is possible, however, is a very reasonable facsimile of such a cellar which is a real tribute to the versatility and flexibility of this unique spirit. Unless malt Scotch is served as an apéritif or a pousse- café, whatever is available can be diluted or "prepared" ahead of time and then decanted as required. At first, this should be done as recommended here. Then let the fun begin and everyone can experiment and do their own thing. For example, as the tastes and textures vary from dish to dish so can the strengths and concentrations be modified from the "stock." The nicest discovery about it all is that one does not have to go through hundreds, even thousands of brands to find just the right taste. There are about ninety distinguishable brands in two strengths and four uisgages (my term for "vintage" which will be explained later).

Building up a cellar might take a little bit of time but, even going through the local liquor board, the limited selections that become available from time to time would allow for a modest but sufficiently wide range of brands to make the result quite interesting. The subtleties would not be there, however, and this is where you might well be able to help your own cause by getting in touch with the closest chapter of **An Quaich**.

Lastly, it will be noted that both terms "malt Scotch whisky" and "malt Scotch" have been used interchangeably. Actually, the term "malt Scotch" is the only correct one inasmuch as the term "Scotch" is synonymous with whisky. It applies to whisky and whisky only. Adjectives and adverbs designating Scotland are "Scot, Scottish, Scots..." and so on. "Scotch" means only one thing - the liquor. However, herein we have used both terms in addition to the single word "malt" which will nevertheless mean, for the purpose of this book, malt Scotch whisky.

You will discover a wonderful new world of enjoyment though your enjoyment may not be as extensive as was mine. After all, there was a lot of "testing" to be done.

To your good health, or as they say in Gaelic, *Slainte mhath!*

BEP

CHAPTER 1
IN THE BEGINNING

A friend of mine asked me recently, "Why are you so fond of malt Scotch?" The question seemed strange and led me to wonder if my enthusiasm about this liquor was being misinterpreted. The negative atmosphere surrounding alcohol in various circles in recent times came to mind very vividly. Reflecting on that question, however, only served to confirm my feelings about this liquor, not to mention my convictions, as well as my gratitude to the gentleman who made the introduction...sooo many years ago now. The answer was not difficult to come by.

It was an unseasonably cold, blustery, early fall evening and there was a fine fire quietly crackling in the hearth in the Officers' Mess. The 30th Field Regiment, Royal Canadian Artillery had been on a "shoot" all day and all of us were due for one of the finer moments of life - the détente after a job well done. Fergus, who well knew my penchant for things traditional, invited me, as we discussed the merits and otherwise of fine wines and liqueurs after Mess Dinners, to share one of his - a "wee dram" of the finest malt Scotch whisky. The rest is history.

Here was a smooth, warm, gentle liquor, not unlike Cognac but not as strong. There was a fruitier quality with a mellower aftertaste. Aaaah! Where had this been all my life? Where could it be obtained? What was it? So many questions - and surprisingly enough, so few answers. There was much more to know about this drink but to my great surprise, very little had or has been written about this liquor compared to wines and beers. Whatever information there was to be had was found in specialty magazines not usually of interest to the general public. This seemed most unfortunate because it struck me that that same public did drink and was being deprived of a most delectable experience. It should be emphasized here and now that we are not talking of the usual blended Scotch whisky of the highball variety but rather the slow sipping liquor that must be nursed along drop by drop, fume by fume.

Curiosity as to the paucity of information got the better of me and part of the answer was found in Michael Brander's book *A Guide to Scotch Whisky* where he explains it quite eloquently:

> A visitor to Scotland may know little else about the country but he, or she, whether rabid teetotaller, or frequent imbiber of alcohol, generally knows that it is the home of Scotch whisky. It is, perhaps, not unusual if his, or her knowledge begins and ends precisely there, for even the Scots themselves are often regrettably ignorant about their national drnk.

The last phrase is a telling one and it is hoped that by means of these pages malt Scotch will become known as much more than the national drink of Scotland - rather, as one of the very finest spirits in the world. Not that everybody might become a Scotch whisky drinker - some have tried it and absolutely hate the stuff. As the French say, "les goûts ne sont pas à discuter" - it is all a matter of taste and not to be questioned.

But two things turned this mere acquaintance into a hobby - firstly, the fact that one could become familiar with all the brands that there are to know, as opposed to the plethora of wines, and therefore become master of the subject much more quickly and thoroughly. The added bonus was that so much more could be learned about the history and customs of a unique area of the world - one of the few repositories of Indo-European customs and expressions as found in Celtic culture. This learning process went much further than what had been originally expected when the use of this fine liquor with food - as it was originally used - was explored, and when the discovery was made of the even more subtle nuances in marrying up the brands with the seasons of the year and even various types of activities.

Inasmuch as wines are associated with France, sherries with Spain, portos with Portugal and beers with Germany, none of these are so readily identified with those countries as Scotch is with Scotland. Probably one of the reasons is that the term "Scotch" itself needs no other label to identify it. Furthermore, no other country is permitted, by law, to produce that liquor and call or sell it by that name. The Scotch whisky that most people know is a blended liquor which has been on the market for barely one hundred years. The single malt is the pure whisky of which all others are made, and as we shall see later, had its origins some 350 years ago in the hills of Scotland as the "water of life" which is the translation of its generic name "uisge beatha" (pronounced oosh'kuh bay'uh). The distillation process used to produce malt is attributed to the Arabs who brought it to Rome. Then the Romans passed it on through France (here is the influence of the Bretons and Normans) and eventually to Scotland.

It is not my intention to go into great detail as to how malt Scotch is produced nor to delve at length into the history of this delightful liquor. There are a number of reference books available and a bibliography is provided at the end of this book. My preference is to open new horizons with regard to taste and the use of this liquor with food. However, since we are dealing with malt whisky as opposed to blends, and since Scotch as a whole is quite different from other liquors, it is desirable to have at least some understanding of the production and make-up of this liquor, in order to appreciate better all of its characteristics. Starting with

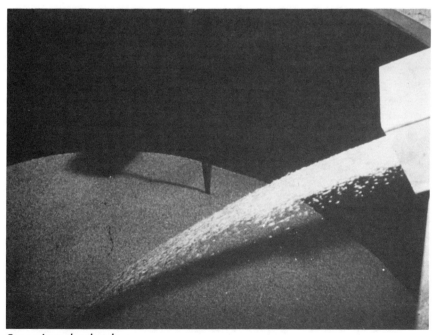

Steeping the barley.

the term "malt," Webster's dictionary has an excellent definition which, for the sake of clarity, is paraphrased hereunder:

> malt is a material obtained by softening grain (as barley or oats) through steeping in water, then allowing it to to germinate in order to develop the enzyme diastase which is capable of turning the starch of the barley or oats into fermentable sugar. The germination process is stopped at the proper time by drying the mash in a kiln. This mash is often ground to a powder (malt) and is used in brewing and distilling as a nutrient and digestive.

In the case of malt Scotch, the material is barley. The steeping lasts for a few days, then the germinating barley is spread evenly on the floor of "malting barns." It is then literally raked every so often during a period of about ten days to ensure that germination is uniform. It takes considerable skill to determine the best moment to stop the germination process so that there is just the right amount of sugar for later fermentation. The arresting process is done by drying the barley over fires fuelled by peat.

Germinating grain being turned over on the malting floor.

Cutting peat from the desolate Scottish moorland.
(Courtesy Scotch Whisky Association, London.)

Fermentation in a 'washback.'

The next step is to mix the malt barley with water at the right temperature to get a good mash so that the water washes away the sugar from the barley. This sweet, non-alcoholic liquid, known as "wort," is drained off into large tubs called "washbacks" where the right amount and type of yeast is added. How such a beautiful liquor can result from such a stinking mess is in itself a mystery, but after a few days of fermentation this liquor is in turn drained and passed through a first distillation in order to obtain a low wine. There is then a second distillation producing a stronger liquor which, however, is still very much undrinkable. This process is the same distillation process learned in high school chemistry and at this stage requires more care than skill in separating the undesirable alcohols from the potable liquor. This liquor is then stored in casks for aging and, after many years, bottled for you and me. The absolute aging time required by law is three years for most malts that will be used for blending. No single malt is sold as such by any self-respecting distiller unless it is at least eight years old.

The essential characteristics of malt Scotch are the mellowness and smokiness imparted at the time that the barley is malting. The starch will absorb the odour and taste of peat and smoke at that time; the amount of absorption is dependent not only on the heat, time and amount of smoke, but also on the absorption qualities of the water. The softer the water, the more the absorption. Fresh water in Scotland is incredibly soft. This faculty for absorption is probably one of the many reasons why the same process manages to produce many different tastes, sometimes in products that are distilled virtually next door. One can now readily appreciate the importance of water, peat, heat, and the smoke that come into play at the malting stage. Yeast, time, and again heat and water are equally important at the fermentation stage.

So much for the malt. The next question that arises usually concerns the difference between single malts, blends and what many refer to as "double malts." The single malt is the pure whisky that results from the process just described. It should be noted that what has just been described is termed the "pot still" process as opposed to the Coffey still process now commonly used for distilling grain alcohols. Speaking of grain alcohols, blends are a mixture of that type of alcohol with one or more single malts. The so-called "double malt" is more properly termed a "vatted" malt and consists of a mixture of two or more single malts. To the purist the "single" malt is the malt resulting from one batch. Any two batches, one following the other then mixed together, result in a "vat" even if they are from the same distillery. In real life, a vatted

The traditional onion shaped 'pot still.'

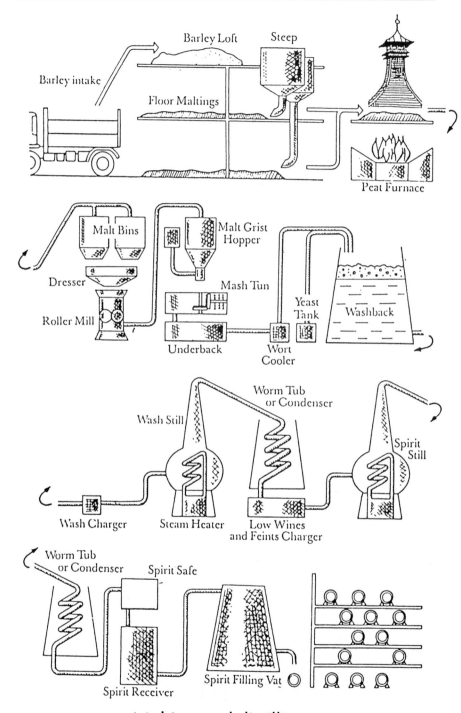

Barley Loft Steep

Barley intake

Floor Maltings

Peat Furnace

Malt Bins Malt Grist Hopper

Dresser

Roller Mill Mash Tun

Underback Wort Cooler Yeast Tank Washback

Wash Still Worm Tub or Condenser Spirit Still

Wash Charger Steam Heater Low Wines and Feints Charger

Worm Tub or Condenser Spirit Safe

Spirit Receiver Spirit Filling Vat

Malting and distilling.
(Courtesy Scotch Whisky Heritage Centre, Edinburgh.)

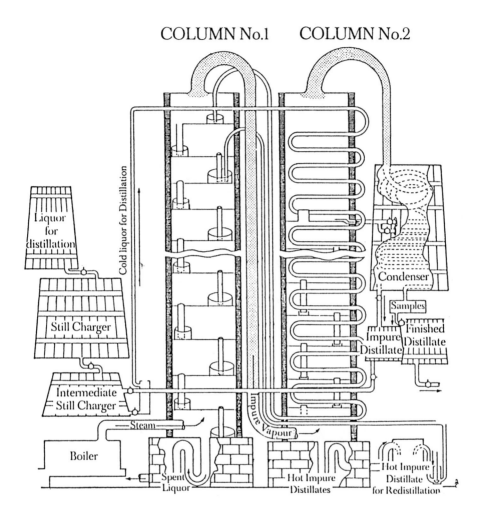

The Coffey Continuous Patent Still.
(Courtesy Scotch Whisky Heritage Centre, Edinburgh.)

malt is usually a mix of a young malt from one distillery, enhanced by blending older malts with different characteristics.

Whether or not such a mixture results in the sum of the best characteristics of each of them is a moot point, but those that were tasted were very interesting, invariably excellent, and somewhat less expensive than a single uisgage.

Where little skill is required in producing grain alcohol, the opposite is true for mixing it with single malts in order to obtain an acceptable blend. Insofar as characteristics are concerned, the grain alcohols, and consequently the blends to a certain extent, have a much harder bite on the tongue. Because malts do get smoother with age, the more malts that are mixed with grain alcohol, and the older the malts, the smoother the blend will be. But the price will consequently be higher because of the number of years that the malts must sleep without being productive. Another phenomenon is that while malt sleeps, quite a bit evaporates through the cask so that the matter of available volume is also worked into the price. Another characteristic to consider is

The skill of blending.
(Courtesy Scotch Whisky Association, London.)

that though grain alcohol has less of the headache producer by-product (fusel oil) than other distillates, the absence of this congeneric element and others is what makes it bland. Herein lies the greatest temptation and practice of adding a mix to the drink, particularly carbonated mixes. Unfortunately this hastens the process of absorption into the blood encouraging anything from a headache to a full-blown hangover.

One would think that with so many variables, it would be easy to explain the differences found in malts but, on the contrary, an analysis of each element does not reveal any explanation or rationale. However, there is little doubt that each element does have a bearing on the end result. There is the element of human intervention at the various stages of distillation and the magic subtlety with which nature works through the hundreds of years in preparing the "soil," in virtually creating genes whereby if a single one were to be modified, a whole new chain would develop. The influence of natural elements gains considerable credibility when one considers the distinct flavours found in the products coming from the four major regions. Variations are found even within each region as in the case of Glenfiddich and Mortlach: so different, yet distilled only a few yards one from the other.

Speaking of regions, it is impossible even to begin discussing malt Scotch without having a good knowledge of the geography. Those that have been set out may differ from the more official ones identified by others but not so much as to be contradictory. The most obvious region and probably best known is the "islands." In many instances one will hear that such and such is an "island" malt when referring to malts from Islay (eye' luh). But that is only one island and there are more, each with at least one brand to its credit. The Orkneys, Skye, Mull and Jura: these are all along the west coast and the very north. Their malts are unmistakable with an iodoform taste and aroma suggesting an influence of sea salt from the prevailing winds. To the south of the imaginary Greenock-Dundee line are the Lowlands with their pale, smooth malts. North of the line and to the east is the Grampian region. To the centre and northwest are the Highlands. To the southwest is the Caledonian region (a new designation that is mine alone). These are all on a variation of the well-rounded, full-bodied theme - but what variations!

There is so much more to say, but to prolong this route would be in bad taste. For this reason, an annotated reference - actually a compilation of available brands and food suggestions - appears in Chapter 15. For those wishing to get more detail on the distillation process, the history of malt Scotch whisky, and foods, there is a select bibliography.

CHAPTER 2
A MATTER OF TASTE

Indeed it is a matter of taste. And as with wines, it is not a matter of pouring it out of the bottle and "down the hatch." That would show a definite lack of couth. There is quite a ritual to tasting and nosing malt Scotch, not unlike the ritual followed by wine tasters throughout the world. But it has been my experience that tasting malt Scotch whisky is much more fun. An intimacy can be achieved with the entire range of the product (well almost), resulting in a more meaningful experience than with wines.

It is unfortunate that the great majority of books written about malt Scotch whisky do not bother to explain the ritual of a good nosing or tasting. Proper nosing and tasting are of the utmost importance, not only to get the most out of money spent by knowing the product being purchased, but particularly important to anybody who, like myself, enjoys malt Scotch whisky at the dinner table.

A lot of fun can be derived from listening to wine tasters "ooooh" and "aaaah" about this brand and that label. How can they really identify characteristics with terms such as "bouquet?" or say that a wine is a "tease?" A bouquet of what? Dandelions, roses, peonies? Surely it is not too difficult to give some kind of identifiable analogy. It's true that whisky tasters also have a vocabulary, but it has considerably more clarity. For example, some malt Scotch whiskys taste and smell like pure iodine straight from the apothecary. Now there's an analogy that cannot be mistaken. Mortlach smells like the bladder of the bagpipe. Another smells like a pair of wet woolen socks. At least it gives a pretty good idea of what the liquid is like even to the rank amateur.

Knowing and recognizing malts is obviously important if they are going to be matched to food. So, as the late comedienne Joyce

Grenfell would have said, "Do let's get on with it and see what nature has given us to play with."

Three senses are involved. They are sight, smell and taste. But before we get all excited and start sipping with our pinkies properly extended, there is one very important element that should be discussed - the tasting vessel. The glass that should be used is a special one. It is better that the glass be thin because then the hands warm up the contents more quickly and keep it that way more easily. The shape is also important and it is generally agreed among afficionados that a stemmed, fluted snifter, narrow at the top and broad at the base, is the best. For the ultimate in a tasting glass, there should be no lip to the rim.

Concerning quantity, the knowledgeable ones agree that half to three quarters of an ounce is quite sufficient. However, if only one sample is being tasted, then why not pay yourself the luxury

The official An Quaich nosing and tasting glass.

of a full ounce and a half. It should be mentioned that, at the end of this book, there is an appendix appendix setting out a tasting form developed by the **AN QUAICH** society and applicable very specifically to malt Scotch.

The great discovery starts with the eyes. The glass is held up to any light or against a pale background (like the table cloth, for example). The idea is to be able to identify as accurately as possible the colour of the liquid. The evaluation of the characteristics is initially undertaken using a scale of one to five. Once proficiency is established, a range of one to ten can be set. That really separates the malts, one from the other. The colour characteristic has a range of amber or gold that goes from light to dark, the light being at 1 and the darker hues having a higher value. One of the darkest to my knowledge is a Macallan 25 years old that would rate a 5+ in my book.

One of the first things that colour will tell you is the type of body the liquor is likely to have. If it has a pale hue the body will tend to be light. A darker colour will generally be associated with a stronger or heavier body. Mark well the use of the word "generally" because there are always exceptions to the rule. The second clue that colour gives about the malt is whether or not it is likely to have been aged in sherry or oak casks. There is a difference - a considerable one - that will affect the colour, taste, and balance.

Casks are not to be taken lightly. They are not just any other container. They are the womb of mother nature wherein this fine amber fluid will gestate for ten, fifteen, even twenty-five years and more. The cask lives and it breathes. Interestingly enough, more has been written about casks and cooperage than about tasting proper. Coopers are nothing short of artists and their product goes a long way in determining the quality of what they contain. Indeed, some distilleries attach so much importance to the nature of the wood, the origin, age, condition and any number of other details associated with casks that what is usually a mere practice or custom becomes a ritual - even a fetish.

For our purposes we will stick to the basics. Whatever I might say about casks would not be original and is already covered quite nicely in McDowall's The Whiskies of Scotland as revised by his son-in-law, William Waugh. He states that sherry casks were always used in the past because they were readily available and inexpensive, having been used to import sherry to England. They

Maturation.   *(Courtesy Scotch Whisky Association, London.)*

contribute a subtle sweetness and impart a darker colour to their contents over the years. Oak bourbon casks are sometimes used, one distiller believing that the charring and the bourbon leaches out the wood flavours, preferring to avoid whatever sherry casks might put into the whisky.

The differences here are the result of the natural process of absorption, breathing and osmosis. In the case of sherry casks, that wood has absorbed appreciable quantities of sherry over the years. Any "woody" tastes that the cask would release into the contents would have been erased long ago with only minute traces of sherry replacing it as the whisky breathes. A virgin cask of oak would understandably release its own taste into the whisky. Without leaching, the taste would be noticeably affected. The leaching process is the eradication of any smoky taste and the implantation of another by natural or artificial processes. Sherry and bourbon are natural processes. Charring is the burning of the interior of the cask. That is where American bourbon (corn mash) acquires its woody taste. Frankly, my preference is for whatever the sherry casks contribute to the whisky rather than what the bourbon does. In general, American oak seems to be preferred in that it absorbs better, and can be "pre-treated" with sherry or used in virgin state to absorb the distinct characteristics of its contents and let nature do its work.

What else can the colour tell us? Ah! The origin. The lighter the colour, the more likely you have a Lowland malt. The medium colours are generally from the Grampian region, and the Island malts are between the mediums and the sherry darks. To recap this point, it could be said that a light colour indicates a Lowland aged in oak. The medium colours would suggest a Grampian/Highland malt aged in oak. A slightly darker colour, say a 3 + to 4, might well be an Island malt in oak. (Island malts are traditionally a bit darker than medium and the aging in oak casks will not affect the colour). It may be a Lowland malt aged in sherry casks (the Lowlands are traditionally light in colour but the sherry casks will darken it). Again, in the slightly darker than medium category, one might find a very old Grampian vatted with any sherry cask aged malt (usually from the same distillery). The 3 + to 4 colour range can give the taster quite a challenge, but - what pleasure!

The darker malts are more likely than not Grampians aged in sherry casks or malts of other regions that have been vatted (mixed - remember?) with an already dark malt and aged further in either oak or sherry casks.

Finally, the very old malts will be darker but not much more than the 3 + if aged in oak casks and maybe a 5 + if aged in sherry casks. On these latter points, only the taste will tell. As far as the Island malts are concerned, these are traditionally a bit darker than the medium amber but on the negative side of 3 +. Vatting does not come into play because, as a class, Island malts are not usually vatted. At least none have been encountered as yet.

Visual analysis will give us yet another clue. Here we refer to the "legs." Malt Scotch whisky legs are something like the streaks of rain on a window pane. However, before we can determine what the legs can tell us, we must know what they are and what causes them. Like the water on the pane of glass, any liquid leaves a story on the surface of the container with which the liquid is in contact. Enter the question of viscosity and surface tension. This can become a very complicated matter in both the realms of physics and chemistry. By definition, surface tension is the tension of the surface of a liquid dependent on molecular forces associated with the phenomena of capillary action. The result is that overall coatings tend to shrink into "legs." By very subtle contrast, the definition of viscosity is the resistance of a fluid to the motion of its molecules among themselves. That subtle difference may be better understood if we consider mercury with very high surface

Legs (tears) formed by surface tension.

tension and virtually no viscosity as compared to molasses with very high viscosity as well as surface tension or cod liver oil, the characteristics of which lie in between. Obviously the viscosity characteristic of molasses is not what is being sought. Therefore, what we are looking for in legs is surface tension, the characteristic that tends to prevent a liquid from spreading. Whether a surface will shrink or spread depends to a large extent on the molecular activity. This in turn is directly related to the hydrogen bonds. These bonds tend to be weak in hydrocarbons - alcohol is one of them. This is the factor that we are looking for. The aging, the water, the yeast, temperature - all these will affect that hydrogen bond. In brief, the surface tension of malt Scotch depends on the amount of starch that is turned into fermentable sugars by the enzyme diastase, the "sleeping" temperature, humidity and aging. Under- standing surface tension leads to the identification of various characteristics. Because the bond is weak there is a natural tendency for alcohol to be runny and careful attention must be given the analysis of this characteristic in order to notice the subtle differences. It also underlines the distiller's skill in knowing when to stop the fermentation of the wet barley. Aging also increases viscosity. The longer the spirit remains in the cask, the more the liquor evaporates leaving a more concentrated, "tighter" mixture. And then, of course, aging in sherry casks also affects the legs along with the colour.

So what do malt Scotch legs tell us? They tell us about the surface tension of the brand in the glass. And, of course, there is a special way of looking at the legs.

First, the glass should be tilted enough so that the liquid reaches about half an inch from the edge. Then the glass should be rolled so that the liquid coats the inside of the glass all around. Now look and see if there is a definite line of demarcation between the dry upper part of the glass and the wet lower portion. The glass should then be held up straight to let the coating run down, just like the water on the pane of glass. Only this time, the liquid should begin separating imperceptibly and gather into streaks, then slowly slide down the inside of the glass. The presence of runny legs indicates low surface tension and a light liquid. The slower the run, and the fewer the number of legs, the more the liquid will resist dispersion and the better the legs. Now the taster has to be very observant to determine the degree of tension because the range with which we are dealing does not exactly run from water to molasses. It should be emphasized that whether the legs are runny or otherwise is no indication of the quality of the liquor. It is simply a clue as to its origin and taste.

Surface tension will also give us some additional clues about the body of the malt Scotch and tell us what to look for when nosing and sipping. At this point we are beginning to combine several sensations and matters become more complex. This is where the fun and challenge of single malt appreciation really begins.

Based on the foregoing, Lowland malts are usually found to be light, the Grampians in the middle and the Island malts with a higher surface tension. The latter is not because of aging necessarily, but is yet another peculiarity of this very special group.

Normally, it would follow then that if a sample is light in colour and has runny legs, it would be a Lowland malt of relatively young age. Similarly, if the colour is medium amber with a certain element of surface tension for the legs, the sample will be a Grampian/Highland malt. If the colour is slightly to the dark of medium with noticeable legs, the chances are that the sample will be an Island malt. Now for the oddball combinations. Suppose that the sample is light in colour but with marked surface tension? It would probably be a light Island malt such as Tobermory, Bowmore or Bunnahabhain. It is interesting that with such little information it is possible to narrow the sample down to possibly three brands. Looking at slightly darker than medium colours and high surface tension, there is another choice of three: Lagavulin, Laphroig and Talisker. The taster can tell these three apart quite readily. Going right along to another combination of dark colour and medium surface tension, the sample would suggest a Grampian sherry cask. And so it goes. But there are exceptions, and it is the discovery of these exceptions that makes the tasting of malt Scotch so interesting.

Now comes the nosing. Some prefer the term "bouquet" but my thoughts have already been expressed on that one! This is not a question of simply sniffing to get an idea of the aroma. Proper nosing will tell much more. To begin, the sample should be warmed by cupping the hands around the glass while gently swirling the liquid. A few minutes should do the trick. The glass should be held upright, the nose brought directly over it and the fumes inhaled deeply. There should be a dry swallow followed by exhalation. Now! What should we look for?

There are three characteristics that are to be identified at the nosing stage. The first is usually termed "attack." This is to determine whether the fumes are sharp to the nose or gentle. The sharpness can be compared to the sting of ammonia. This particular characteristic raises considerable discussion among tasters. Some will contend that if the fumes are sharp and sting, then it must mean that the elements going into the sample have had time to concentrate with age and that the sample comes from a mature batch. Others will say that the sting is due to youth and that the liquid has not had the chance to mix properly and evaporate through the wood. In other words, as with ammonia, the vapours are fresh and strong. The preferred interpretation here is that fresh alcohol is sharper and age does smooth out the sting. Be mindful that the attack carries its own message, one that can be only fully understood and appreciated when taken in context with the other two characteristics of the nosing, "presence" and "persistence."

Presence is another term for "awareness" of body. When the fumes of the sample are inhaled, if there is presence, there is no mistaking it. Contrary to the sting, presence may be light or strong. This presence may be quite powerful but it is not a stinging sensation, as in the analogy of ammonia. A presence will be light if an aroma, any aroma, is barely noticeable or is very subtle. A presence will be strong if there is a definite smell of something, be it the iodine, the woolen socks, or the bagpipe bladder. Again the Lowland malts tend to have a light and airy presence. On the other hand, the Island malts are readily recognized for their iodine-like presence.

The amount or extent of the awareness is not the only element of this characteristic; there is also the aroma, and whereas the awareness could be measured in strength, the aroma should be measured in weight. A subtle, light fragrance of "je ne sais quoi," as the eonophiles would say, is indicative of a Lowland malt. A medium-weight aroma with neither the smell of smoke nor peat indicates a well-balanced Grampian sample. These include the better known brands such as THE Glenlivet, Glenfiddich, Milton-Duff, Dufftown and Glendronach (original) among others. A medium-weight presence with a light-weight aroma would indicate something like a Cardhu, whereas a slightly heavier presence with an aroma that is woody with the smell of neither peat nor smoke nor iodine is a good indication of something like the Clynelish or the Dalmore. A presence that is gentle and heavy is more an indication of age and must be considered with other elements in order to have any merit for identification purposes. Needless to say that the heavier and more pervasive the presence, then the older the uisgage. Now that's a term that nobody has even heard of until a few pages ago and it gives me great pleasure to introduce it as my candidate for the term denoting "year" or "age" for malt Scotch whisky, much as "vintage" is used for wine. The suggested pronounciation using Gaelic rules gives "oosh-k'ej."

Back to the presence. The last category to consider is the medium to strong cloaked with a definite mellow aroma. If the colour is dark, you have a dead give-away for a sherry cask uisgage. The Macallan and Glendronach (sherry) are the classics of this type.

Along with the weight of the presence, the uisgage can be detected by the staying power of the nose. Again, once having inhaled and dry swallowed the fumes of the sample, if on a second swallow there is nothing there, then the sample is light and volatile. This would probably be a Lowland malt. You can now probably also speculate that the greatest staying power would be with the Island malts. Quite right but not exclusively.

Sight and smell have done just about all they can and there remains but one more of the senses to call upon for the full appreciation of Alba's ambrosia. It is the long-awaited moment, the tasting. Whereas the visual evaluation and the nosing can take as long as fifteen minutes and maybe longer depending on the depth and extent to which one wishes to go, the tasting can be even longer. Most readers will be familiar with the method of tasting wine by swirling a mouthful and spitting out the sample. The swirling is quite acceptable but it is absolutely not my intention to part with even a molecule of malt Scotch - at any time. Not that it is so expensive, but if we are going to taste then taste we should, and the tasting does not stop at the mouth. The stomach has something to say about it, as does the throat. Mind you, it is easy to understand the claim made by purists that a good comparison can only be made if the olfactory system remains untainted. That is why many rinse out the mouth and eat a piece of white bread or Scottish oat cakes between samples. But if you insist, we can do the same. Maybe with wine it is not difficult to "cleanse" the mouth, but after even a wee dram of Laphroig, it will take some doing before the lining of the mouth and nose are back to neutral. What does help, is to sample very little and let a bit of time and saliva do the neutralizing. So much for the preliminary comments. Now for the tasting.

This is a bit more complicated because we are now looking at five different characteristics strictly associated with taste. They are body, bite, smoke, peat, and aftertaste, more easily remembered by the initials B B S P A. The two other senses can also be remembered by the initials C L A P P (recalling colour, legs, attack, presence and persistence). Most connoisseurs agree that the after-taste is most important — something like the actual taste of a cheese as compared to its smell. Something very important to malt Scotch tasting is that it is accomplished in two phases. The first is the savouring of the sample in its pure form and the other is tasting it with a drop or two of water added. The latter does some strange things like loosening up the material and making the identification of characteristics a little easier. The only other liquor where this process is used in tasting, to this writer's knowledge, is with brandies, particularly Cognac.

Many would suggest that the tasting with the water should come first and this would be reasonable were it not for the second dose of whisky then required, because once the sample is diluted, there is no other way you can taste it in its pure state. Also, the fact remains that if the first sip is of the pure product, it may well dull the senses for the diluted sample. With both the numbness and the dilution, the exercise will be less than satisfactory. If it's a

Looking for the colour and the legs.

matter of economy then use the water last. If you can go for two drams then go with the water first. In any case, you are looking for the same things, keeping in mind that the characteristics are bound to be more subtle. The diluted sample will provide a definite confirmation of what was found in the pure liquor.

The ritual commences with a sip, a swirl, and a half swallow. Fumes are then passed through the nose. What has gone down the throat and into the stomach is now well heated up along with the remainder of the sample in the mouth. Those fumes will tell a lot. It is good to have a pencil handy to note the body, bite, smoke, peat, and aftertaste. That is phase one. Phase two involves swallowing what is left in the mouth followed by a rubbing of the palate with the tongue. Again note the characteristics. Most will be perceived quite handily with the exception of the aftertaste. This is not a matter of difficulty but rather a matter of time. This is phase three and requires another little sip swallowed slowly, followed by a deep breath and a few very slow and gentle dry swallows. Ahaa! What is it that lingers on and on and on, hopefully...?

After all this, what have we found? The identity of an obscure brand? If you can tell the difference between any more than ten or fifteen, you are a true connoisseur and need very little advice, if any. If it's any consolation, experts of this calibre exist only among the blenders and even they have their limits. To be able to distinguish one brand from a large sampling of others the taster must be exceptionally familiar with at least one of the samples. That means no less than ten to fifteen years of living, smelling and possibly drinking that brand only.

First we are looking for the body. Since we are sending fumes through the nasal passage, some of the comments in the nosing would apply here. Do we have something? Is there a taste to match the fragrance? Are we drinking coloured water or is it a concentrate? Whatever it is, is it there? If not, give it a 1; if so, then anything from a 3 to a 5. Indeed! The Lowlands get the lighter ratings and the Island malts get the 5s, again with exceptions.

Next, the bite. Remember the attack with its sting? The bite is the same thing only in the mouth. Remember also what we said about alcohol, that though it does not smell or have any colour, there is one dandy reaction in contact with the buccal membranes: burning bite, young brew. Now, of course, we must understand each other and remember that malt Scotch at cask strength has a very respectable amount of alcohol. So, by its very nature, it is going to burn and that is why we can't judge by the bite alone. On this point, the aftertaste is most important.

Peat and smoke almost speak for themselves. If neither can be detected then the sample is well-balanced. This in no way suggests that an unbalanced malt Scotch whisky is not good. Remember! It's a matter of taste. The amount of balance or imbalance one way or the other will simply give a clue as to the identity and, of course, with what it should be served at the dinner table!!! The Lowland malts are usually exceptionally well-balanced.

In my opinion, and you may well agree once you have reached the appendices of this book, the Lowland malts, slightly diluted, are about the best to serve at the dinner table in general terms. They will blend with and/or enhance any dish in a very subtle way. To get a real balance or enhancement, as we shall see later, we have to go to a different area, but unless it's something special, in taste that is, take a Lowland and you can't go wrong. It is hoped that this paragraph will dispel any notion that my opinion of the Lowland malts is not very high. On the contrary.

And now for what is considered to be the supreme test - the aftertaste. This is where the initial reactions are confirmed or dispelled. The aftertaste will be either sharp or mellow and fleeting or persistent. When first tasted, a sample may have seemed light and biting but in the aftertaste, the initial bite will slowly change to something quite a bit more mellow. By the same token, what appeared fleeting to the nose and the taste may now show considerable staying power. The ritual also involves constant rubbing of the tongue against the palate and slow exhalation, letting the fumes, now from the stomach, do their job on the taste buds and the nasal membranes.

Understanding what creates these qualities partially unravels the mystery of why two malts, distilled in the same tradition with virtually the same ingredients, merely a few yards from each other, will have such different tastes. THE Glenlivet and Mortlach are the prime examples of this phenomenon.

In the final analysis, the aftertaste shows that the sample with the staying power is older than the fleetier one and the mellowness will confirm the nature of the aging cask as well as the age and the region of origin. At one time, when the barley was home grown, this clue was much more accurate than it is now. Another clue uncovered by the mellowness is the water. Though all the water in Scotland is very soft, there are areas that are softer than others and the surrounding terrain, as will be discussed later, may have a lot to do with it. Thus the importance of the subtle ritual of aftertaste.

Should there be a summary with clues as to brands? Not really. But what you, the reader, should do is to start compiling the characteristics of as many samples as you can get, and, using the evaluation sheet in the appendices, fill in the remarks area with your own comments. Most important of all, try your samples with the various foods that are discussed later on...and do enjoy!

CHAPTER 3
THE CHEMISTRY
OF MALT SCOTCH WHISKY

This chapter will not enter into any deep chemical discourse about the elements that constitute malt Scotch whisky, nor is it intended to become involved with the distillation process. However, the elements that make up or influence this alcoholic beverage indicate that at least a basic understanding of these factors and their relationship with human physiology commends itself to our attention.

After having courted malt Scotch whisky for nigh on to forty years, I feel it can be said with little fear of contradiction that it is an alcoholic beverage quite different from any of its brethren. This difference is readily noticeable by the taste and smell - but that is barely scratching the surface. It goes much deeper than that. My first clue was the absence of the traditional hangover "the morning after the night before," though more than my usual quota had been consumed, which in any event is not very much. This was indeed interesting. At this juncture a caveat is entered NOT to go out and guzzle the next bottle of Glenwhatever before ALL of this chapter has been read and understood. Malt Scotch is still very much an alcoholic beverage!

No properly distilled potable alcoholic beverage is harmful in itself if consumed moderately. But alcohol is alcohol and it must be treated with respect - in the case of malt Scotch it should be treated with admiration as well as respect. This "revelation" came to me after I had undertaken a bit of research into alcohol. In fact, it is firmly believed, as a result of this research, that with more knowledge about this substance and an intelligent education program, there might be less abuse and attendant costs. There would be much rejoicing if this chapter alone would begin to open that door. Indeed, when viewed critically, every substance has an intrinsic nature which is either good or bad. Even the good, when abused, has undesirable consequences. Not being a chemist or a physiologist, my comments will be restricted to what is obvious and to what has been gleaned from learned writings. Kindly note, however, that even water, when abused, can alter the electrolytic balance of blood so as to cause shock and death. The same can be said of many well-known headache remedies.

About four hundred years before the birth of Christ, some ingenious character discovered that capturing the cooled vapours of just about anything in sight that had been mixed with water produced something quite different from the original material. Experimentation naturally led to alcohol and who knows how many died finding out what part of what brew was potable and which was not? Eventually, the proper recipe for producing potable alcohol through distillation was found. The danger that remains, however, may best be illustrated by the fact that some individuals still die from "bath-tub gin."

The alcohol of interest to us is not intrinsically harmful (as are some other alcohols which are outright poisons), but this is because its production follows very strict rules. It can be very harmful when abused. To my great joy, and hopefully yours, it is not as injurious as other liquors of similar ilk. As a start, we should look at the nature of alcohol as a genus, if only to realize that the line on which we

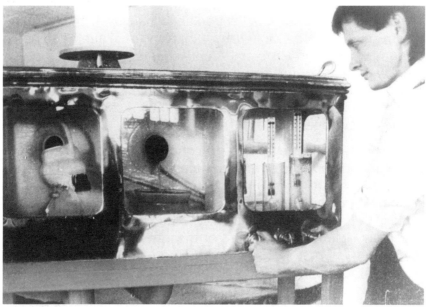

The spirit safe.   *(Courtesy Edradour Distillery, Pitlochry.)*

walk when we drink alcohol is oh! so very fine. Alcohols are in the chemical family of hydro-carbons and therefore the distillation of any hydro-carbon mash produces alcohol so long as the mash is heated at just the right temperature to produce vapours. For those liquors that we wish to consume, we use mash from grains and fruits. If we used wood, for example, we would wind up with wood alcohol, a pure poison. As it is, the importance of selecting the best alcohol cannot be overstressed and therein lies the importance of separating the foreshots and aftershots or feints from the quality liquid as it passes through the spirit safe. That is the distiller's quick way of saying that, as the low wine is distilled, the first "conden-sations," otherwise known as the foreshots must be separated, as must the last condensations, from the middle condensations. The reason is that the foreshots and feints contain traces of what we know as turpentine, nail polish, shaving lotion, anti-freeze, paint remover and so on. Please remember that this applies to any alcohol. Needless to say, a healthy respect for this liquid has been developed and virtually all types have been eliminated from my diet with the exception of malt Scotch - and some blends. Here's why.

As mentioned previously, a given temperature will produce vapours of a given product. That is why temperature control is critical in every phase of whisky production, particularly distilla-tion. If raw potable alcohol is redistilled two or three times, a very pure product results with no taste whatsoever. Therefore, to produce a marketable product there must be a compromise between creating the best liquor possible while leaving only those by-products that will produce the most desirable taste. It is these taste-producing by-products that contain elements, minuscule though they may be, of those undesirables mentioned above. Ah - the skill of the stillmen! And the trust that we place in them. Further considering the softness of Scottish water and its incredible absorption qualities, no wonder there is such a range of flavours for a proportionate content of congeners as are found in other spirits.

To produce whisky we must first ferment the mash. If we stop there, we get beers and wines. At this stage, many congeners or congeneric by-products are contained in the liquid. In the case of malt Scotch, this liquid is then distilled at least twice to reduce the congeners and give us an acceptable product. It must be remem-bered that because of the absorption qualities of the water, proportionally more taste will remain compared to any other liquid for the same reduction of congeneric content. In the same class of distillates we find Cognac and Bourbon, but the number and types of "rectifications" are not that different. Why then is malt Scotch so different - even within its own family? The answer is that Bourbon is made from corn mash and aged in charred maple casks and Cognac is a distillate of wine. Though a chemical analysis reveals little difference in congeneric content, other factors that greatly favour malt Scotch are the method of distillation (using the pot still), the raw materials, an acid-free environment, and absence of charcoal and chemical additives, as well as a very different pH factor.

Not surprising then that it is called uisge beatha or water of life - like so many others today such as Aquavit or the French Eau Vie. Indeed, in St. Paul's words to Timothy, as first noted above, "No longer drink only water, but use a little wine for the sake of your stomach and your frequent ailments." Kindly note the admonition "...use a little..." The moderate user will find alcohol relaxing and a shy person may feel less inhibited. However, when alcohol is used to the exclusion of more realistic means to meet life situations, or if alcohol is relied upon to remove anxiety and overcome difficulties, then the danger signs are there.

The chemistry of alcohol and therefore malt Scotch has a very particular interaction with food, quite foreign to the aspect of taste. Gene Ford in his book *The Benefits of Moderate Drinking* has a truck load of reports confirming that all "alcoholic beverages should be taken with food." In this respect, we can better appreciate the advantages of "munchies" at cocktail parties. But what we are after are the advantages of real food.

A great deal has been said about wine at the dinner table but nothing about malt Scotch. Yet that was one of its first uses. And a good one. As a starter - and as a matter of taste - no malt liquor will have the acetic characteristic of wine. This acetic taste is more telling than one realizes. For example there is the matter of sour stomach, the feeling of "the morning after," lethargy, and so on. Mention has already been made of the congeneric elements in beers, wines and spirits as the malaise producers. This is fine when you have only the congeners to contend with, but in the case of wines we must not forget the chemical additives that are now very much part of the standard production. Not so with malt Scotch. An interesting point is made by Mendelson in one of his studies with Mello on alcohol and congeners, stating that distilled spirits, which have a higher congeneric content than wine, will be absorbed more slowly...Aha! Remember what was said about the congeners in malt Scotch and the lesser concentration required to impart taste due to the softness of Scottish waters. We now have a double- barrelled reason for at least giving malt Scotch a shot at the dinner table.

The physiology of alcohol should be given at least a cursory glance in order to appreciate more fully its association with the following chapter - Malt Scotch Whisky and Food. We often wonder why alcohol affects us the way it does, both as an appetite stimulant and social relaxant. To find out, we should follow the path alcohol takes once swallowed.

Alcohol passes from the mouth to the stomach where small amounts are absorbed depending on the amount of food that is already there. Do remember it is only very small amounts which are absorbed in the stomach, principally because alcohol is not digested and then also because of the amount of food already there. More than ninety percent of the alcohol is passed by the small intestines directly into the bloodsstream. This occurs without digestion or any other chemical change of alcohol. It could be termed a process similar to osmosis whereby oxygen passes from the lungs' alveoli through the walls to the blood in exchange for carbon dioxide. Here there is no exchange. The amount of alcohol transmitted to the blood in this manner is the residue of whatever the liver cannot handle. It is the liver that breaks down alcohol into its constitutents of water, carbon dioxide, and energy. Since the liver can take back in from the blood slightly over half an ounce of absolute alcohol every hour, the remaining alcohol continues to circulate.

The primary impact of alcohol in the bloodstream occurs in the brain and on the central nervous system. Ford further suggests that this is demonstrated on both the emotional and autonomic levels. Depression of the central nervous system produces what is known as the "release" phenomenon. This state often sets off a heightened physical activity and excess vitality in the short run. Appetite is generally stimulated because the mouth and stomach acids flow more freely. Research has shown that the healthful effect of alcohol in this type of drink is achieved by the relaxation of the walls and the resultant dilation of blood vessels serving the "autonomic" organs, specifically those concerned with nutritive, glandular, vascular and other physiological activities. This means that blood pressure is lowered and that there is an easier flow of blood to these organs. Senses are keener and function is improved. Once alcohol has reached the circulatory system its origin is not important. Beer, wine, vodka, Scotch - all will have the same impact.

The pleasurable or relaxing aspect is more insidious and we should realize that though food helps in slowing down absorption, many other factors come into play. However, once alcohol enters the bloodstream, it travels around and around the body relentlessly until it is completely oxidized by the liver. In the meantime, it is to be noted that ethanol, which is the generic name for our alcohol, does not remain in the cells or tissue as a foreign deposit. Lipids are one of the main constituents of all cell walls or cell membranes. To travel from the bloodstream into the brain, then into the nerve cells, alcohol has to pass through cell walls. The alcohol molecule is unique in the ease with which it can enter nerve cells and return to the blood. Thus can the brain cells be so quickly affected.

Two questions have often been asked of me: how does the stupor or anaesthetized state occur, and why. The best and simplest analogy is that the brain is similar to a transmitter relying on electrical impulses to send messages to the muscles through the nerves. In this instance the nerves are the wires and the muscles are the receptors be they bells, lights, little motors, whatever. There is an element in alcohol that acts as an insulator. It seeps into the wire where it is connected to the transmitter (brain) and prevents the impulses from getting through. Then slowly, just as air will cause a wet spot to evaporate, oxygen will, with time, cause the insulating material to dissipate and the connection will be reestablished. If, however, there is too much of that insulating material, then the very nature of the wire will be changed and the damage will be severe or even permanent.

Ethyl alcohol, or ethanol for our purposes, is not a foreign substance, but a natural chemical produced within the body every day. Referring to yet another passage from Ford, the make-up and proper functioning of our own body is such that it produces alcohol naturally in the same way that it manufactures the enzymes required to break down alcohol into its energy and waste components. The metabolizing of the alcohol molecule is accomplished in the liver by the action of enzymes and coenzymes, principally by alcohol dehydrogenase. When an imbalance exists or develops that the body cannot handle, there is trouble ahead. Luckily food can help - and that's next.

At this juncture, the matter of grain alcohol should also be discussed, though with some reluctance - no matter how briefly - because the subject matter is really malt Scotch. Nevertheless, because questions were, are and probably will always be asked about the relationship of blends and grain alcohol to malt Scotch, the following should put the matter to rest. A blend is a mixture of malt Scotch whisky and grain alcohol. The question then remains, how is grain alcohol made and how do blends really differ from malts? Also, why do blends exist at all?

To make a long story short, there are blends because grain alcohol is much cheaper to produce than malt Scotch. Grain alcohol has no taste. Mix the two together and the result is a Scotch whisky (blend) that is less expensive yet has some of the taste of the malt. In fact, some blends contain quite a number of malt brands but these tend to be more expensive and, to be truthful, even experts can be fooled as to whether a sample is a blend or a "neutral" malt Scotch whisky. So much for the "why."

Insofar as the difference between a blend and a malt Scotch whisky is concerned, we have already delved a little bit into that. The distinction to be made deals more with the biophysiological aspects. Reference has already been made to the fact that the fewer congeners there are in ethanol, the more quickly it is absorbed into the blood stream. Well then, add straight ethanol to malt Scotch whisky and the rate of absorption increases - right? Then, as was stated before, some individuals go and add soda or some other carbonated material and augment the absorption rate yet again.

Lastly, one may wonder how grain alcohol is made. The answer is that it can be made in the pot still just like malt Scotch whisky, but the results are obtained much more quickly using the Coffey patent still, invented by Aeneas Coffey, Inspector General of Excise for Ireland around 1830. Also, instead of using barley, grain alcohol is produced from wheat, rye or maize. Whisky authority Derek Cooper in his book The Century Companion to Whiskies states, "...the advantage of the patent still is that it can be used twenty-four hours a day, seven days a week. No need for silent seasons, no need to clean out the still after each wash. Furthermore, patent stills can be sited, as most of them are to-day, in towns because they do not rely on cold, burn (stream) water."

For the distillation process I turn to Michael Brander. Barley is steeped and malted in Saladin boxes just as it would be in the pot still process and is then dried in oil fired kilns. No peat is introduced at any stage. The bulk of the starch needed for the mash comes from the maize which is ground into a fine consistency and cooked at high temperatures so that every particle can be exposed for conversion by the diastase of the malt into sugar.

The barley and malt maize are mixed with hot water, stirred for a few hours until the starch has turned into sugar and then the contents of the mash "tun" are allowed to settle. The cereals fall to the bottom and the saccharine water or wort is pumped up to the refrigerators where it is cooled before being run to the fermenting vessels or washbacks. Yeast is added and fermentation takes place. After fermentation the liquid is pumped into the still. The patent still consists of two large cylindrical copper columns about forty feet high with pipes at the top so that the cold liquid goes down through a coil in the first cylinder. This is a simple way of cooling the contents of the first cylinder which has just returned from the second cylinder through a pipe at the bottom.

The liquid inside the coil reaches the bottom of the first cylinder and, now being warm, rises through a pipe attached to the top of the second cylinder. The inside of this second cylinder has a series of perforated plates or platforms through which steam is pumped from the bottom. The liquid meets the upward jet of steam rising through the perforated plates. Since alcohol boils and evaporates at a lower temperature than water, as the wash slowly drips downwards through each succeeding compartment, the alcohol rises with the steam. The steam is diverted into the base of the first cylinder, called the rectifier, and continues to rise steadily being cooled by the cooler wort being pumped down the coils. By this method, the purest alcohol rises to the top while the heavier impure higher and lower alcohols condense lower down, having a yet lower boiling point. They are then drawn off for re-distillation and the end result is nearly pure alcohol.

Grain whisky must also be aged - at least for three years. Though the purist will never admit it, if barley mash is taken and put through the patent still and then aged in casks for the usual time, the end product will not be very different from the Highland malt. In fact this process is used in the Lowlands. The patent still removes many of the congeners found in pot still whisky and consequently when it is reduced with water and put into casks it is altogether milder and requires less time to mature. This is not to say that it is better, and milder is not necessarily smoother.

CHAPTER 4
MALT SCOTCH WHISKY AND FOOD

To say that nothing has been written about Scotch whisky and food would be wrong and totally unfair to the late Dione Pattullo, a leading Scottish cookery author. She collaborated with Derek Cooper in giving ideas for whisky cocktails, punches and liqueurs and the marrying of Scotch with many foods.

What has been written, however, deals with the use of Scotch in cooking as opposed to its consumption with what has been cooked. It is my intention to deal with both, though in the case of the former, mine will be more of a commentary than a treatise with any claim to originality. Indeed, to be original where cooking is concerned would be difficult because, as Theodora FitzGibbon puts it, Scotland's ties with the home of great cooking, France, go back as far as Charlemagne in the ninth century.

It is impossible to resist the next comment taken from her book with Derek Cooper, *Enjoying Scotch,* that "many Scottish dishes are French in origin, but adapted to Scottish tastes and ingredients. Whisky is, in fact, a much purer spirit than brandy and so can successfully be used in its place in many recipes." So much for those who wish to compare malt Scotch whisky to brandy, or Cognac for that matter.

Iris Price Jones puts it another way in her book on Celtic Cookery and compares the fruits of the sea and the land that are common to Scotland and Brittany.

Most of the sources consulted in researching this book all agree that in the early days, malt Scotch was not only as common as water but in many instances took its place. It bears repeating that it was very much part of the dinner table and according to Dr. McDowall, writing in *The Whiskies of Scotland,* was also quite often recommended as a medicine. Why then do we now know it mostly as a social drink? And why do we hear mostly about the

The combinations are unlimited.

blends - so little about the malts? Derek Cooper in his work *Century Companion to Whiskies* puts it in the form of another question, "Scotch - luxury or necessity?"

He states that the Scots have more than ample reason to rebel against the discriminatory amounts of duty levelled on their national drink. After setting out tables comparing the price of Scotch to other spirits he continues that today, more than ever, a dram has been priced out of the everyday reach of many Scots who pay thrice the duty on their whisky that the Englishman pays on his bitter.

The same research revealed that many countries and regions within a country collaborate in procuring and maintaining the best products at reasonable prices. The United States, France and Italy are prime examples. But many governments are adept at spotting good tax sources when they see them and in this respect, Canadian and British consumers do not fare very well. In Canada, for example, a case of twelve 750 ml bottles of average malt Scotch costs $60.00 (Cdn) FOB Scotland, but when that same case reaches the Canadian consumer, the price tag has reached $384.00!!! And the original $60.00 includes the distiller's profit. Is it any wonder that we are so far away from the Scottish Nirvana of selections. However, the picture seems to be changing ever so slowly, mostly thanks to modern society's increased affluence. In spite of this improvement, Chapter 14 illustrates so many other shortcomings in the whole approach by both government and industry that the reader will readily understand the raison d'être of **An Quaich**. A proper program of understanding imposes itself.

Another reason for the virtual dearth of malt Scotch brands is that blends, as mentioned before, are not nearly so expensive. Since they sell better, there is a greater profit for all concerned. The result is that agents, distillers, and anybody else other than the consumer are much more interested in promoting the money producer rather than promoting the expensive product.

This is an unforgivable error, because ounce for ounce, one cannot begin to compare the quality of malt Scotch with the great majority of blends. Furthermore, if malt is diluted to "table strength," it is less expensive than its wine counterpart. As a liqueur it is also less expensive than other spirits of equal age and quality.

The versatility of this spirit more than rivals its grape juice cousin. Kindly note that any dish in French cuisine that is flambé makes use of brandy (a distillate of wine) and many sauces of the exquisite variety have recourse to wine for enhancement. Malt Scotch handles both those chores with remarkable insouciance. The point is easily made in paraphrasing Dione Pattullo once again who suggested that, when using whisky as a cooking ingredient, most shellfish react quite favourably to it. Do remember that we are now talking of using Scotch (blends) for cooking and not as the table companion to food. The present commentary is intended to show that if a Scotch blend enhances cooking, its malt brother can well be expected to do wonders with the end product.

It should be emphasized that when mention is made of Scotch at the table, only the malts are intended and not the blends. A similar distinction is imperative where cooking is concerned. Dione Pattulo made this point by suggesting that only inexpensive blends should be used. Of course, if you prefer to use the real material the results will show. Consequently, any flavouring by the cook will have to be all the more judicious. Also, the cost will be very much evident.

Once the acquaintance with malt Scotch has been made, it does not take too much imagination to understand how this fine liquor might enhance food, be it in the cooking thereof or as a table drink. It enhances the flavour of game birds and particularly the tasteless pheasant. Malt Scotch has its place with beef, pork, lamb, and in the marinade for game pies and pâtés. Sweet dishes on the other hand tend to react differently to the flavour of malt Scotch and need a different approach. Much as there are numerous wines and vinegars for various dishes, so do we have a selection of malt whiskies for specific culinary preparations. On the whole, puddings and sweet dishes are best made with malt Scotch, keeping the cost in mind of course. In order to prevent disastrous results, care must also be exercised in selecting the appropriate brand for sweet dishes. It would also be quite wasteful to use an expensive malt in sauces when an inexpensive blend would do. This is particularly so in the case of sauces with a character of their own.

The foregoing barely scratches the surface of our research in the kitchen and in the libraries. Seafood, fowl, meats, cheeses, desserts...one discovery led to another...and another...and another. Disappointments? Indeed, there were some dandies. Quite naturally, the question came to mind, "is there really a malt Scotch for every type of dish?" The answer had to be a resounding "yes." And there are as many Scotch whiskies for one dish as there may be dishes for one Scotch. Moreover, distilleries augment and then reduce the number of brands available from year to year. Therein lies another challenge of marrying an uisgage to a favourite dish - and never wandering very far from a common comparison base within a relatively restricted range of brands. Many of the distilleries produce more than one uisgage and a number of others go dormant for an extended period of time. Others close, supposedly on a permanent basis while yet others reopen periodically. For our purposes we have selected some eighty-five brands which are readily available and which cover the gamut of tastes. Though there are many more available in Scotland, the eighty-five selected represent the equivalent of an intimate knowledge of some two hundred wines for the eonophile - quite an accomplishment. Furthermore, those wines would not have the same scale or variety of tastes as the malt Scotch whiskies. How can this be so? Elsewhere in these pages, it is stated that the taste range of malt Scotch whiskies embraces the wine equivalent of whites and reds from Bordeaux and Burgundy, the secs of Alsace, the Niersteiners and Rieslings, the raw reds of Chianti, the sharp Amontillados and the sweet sherry creams as well as the heavy portos of Malaga. Those and all the ones in between make for an impressive range...and the malts have them all.

"Where are these gems to be found?" you ask. Firstly, there are four generally recognized classifications of brands which correspond to specific geographical areas of Scotland. There are the Lowlands ,which lie south of an imaginary line between Dundee and Greenoch and cover that area from east to west. The Highlands are north of the Greenoch-Dundee line and east of another line drawn from Greenoch to Inverness. A "pocket" south of the Caledonian Canal is responsible for the Campbeltown malts, now virtually extinct. The island malts originate from the islands of Skye, Islay, Jura, Mull and Orkney. Within the first three areas or categories there are well recognized regions and these are equally well defined in the accompanying map. The characteristics vary sufficiently within each region to be of significance but to list them here would be more confusing than of value. Suffice it to say that they will be properly identified at the appropriate time.

One naturally might get the idea that island malts would go well with seafood, and that idea is quite correct. Likewise, the central Highland malts would tend to go well with meats. Again quite close to true. But there are variations on this theme such that the above can only be a very broad rule of thumb at best. With this in mind, one last comment. As has been stated so many times before, all of this is a matter of taste for each and every individual. What may be pleasing to one may be a disaster to another. Only experience can be your ultimate guide. Experimenting was always most enjoyable, particularly when undertaken in the context of a project. It is hoped that you will have as much fun. What follows is a starting point.

CHAPTER 5
BEFORE DINNER, THE APERITIF

More and more people are recognizing the benefactions of a pre-dinner drink commonly known as the aperitif. The aperitif is designed to whet the appetite and set the mood for the meal. While many individuals attach a lot of importance to the selection of a wine to enhance a meal, few attach the same importance to the selection of the aperitif, going by preference of taste alone and not paying attention to its propriety with the meal to follow. A great number of individuals know only the blended Scotch and regard it as a highball. They are quite unaware that the malt Scotch is not only an excellent dinner drink, like wine, but is an equally good aperitif - probably the best of all. However, the selection must be judicious because of the "carry-over" taste of the aperitif into the meal.

Firstly, many so-called aperitifs have a strong taste of their own and while they may well whet the appetite, they will not enhance the taste of the food or the mood of the occasion. One of the reasons is that the nature of the aperitif and the nature of the traditional dinner drink, wine, are so different. But such is not the case with malt Scotch whisky when it is used both as aperitif and dinner drink. Careful though! The brands should not be so different as to fall into the same situation as cocktail versus wine. The brand or brands offered as apéritif should be such as to marry well with the brand at the meal - the one that governs. Any meal will then truly be a memorable occasion.

Secondly, the brand of malt Scotch selected as an aperitif depends not only on the food that is to follow, but as much on the season of the year, the temperature and mood or atmosphere of the room, and the activity in which one has just partaken. If this appears to be stretching things a bit too much, then bear these comments in mind the next time you have the opportunity of trying it out. Most important, however, always remember that an aperitif is a pre-dinner drink and therefore the selection should match what follows the aperitif, the food.

The general (and the word "general" is very much emphasized) rule for the main course is that the Island malts usually go well with strong fish and wild red "gamey" meats. The less "gamey" the red meats, the more one tends towards the traditional Highland or Grampian malts These same traditional Grampians also go well with small game such as rabbit and hare. Lowland should usually be reserved for fowl with the exception of the "gamey" ones such as pheasant at which time a stronger-bodied malt such as the Campbeltown (my Caledonian) malts should be selected. These malts also go well with white fish and mussels. Last but certainly not least are the dishes where oats and oatmeal play a large part. These are usually enhanced by lower Grampian and Lowland malts which shall be discussed later. Of course, there are variations on this theme, and since taste is always a matter of personal preference, this is but a rule of thumb - for the aperitif.

The above is all well and good if the cellar is one that offers such a choice. Then it is important to be thoroughly familiar with what is going to wind up on the table. If you are preparing for a special occasion, no doubt the meal itself will be geared to any foregoing activity such as hiking, fishing, shooting, a hunt, and so

The pause before. . .

on. The selection of the libation is then less complicated. On the other hand, if there is no meal at all, the matter is quite simple and the aperitif, in this case the "drink," should be geared to the activity, the season, weather and mood. Important? You bet. Watch...

In warm weather, the Lowland malts are generally better received, particularly if the malt itself has been chilled. Though many purists will not tolerate anything in the glass other than the malt itself, some concession is to be made to distilled water. This is quite acceptable considering the temperature or the weather. A lump of ice is also acceptable. One must be very careful, however, because the chilled malt can be incredibly smooth with a lingering aftertaste. The danger is that one may tend to sip a little faster than usual - with some rather unusual effects.

At the risk of being called a heretic, there is something that must be said at this juncture. It has been claimed by many that malt Scotch must be imbibed in its pure state with no water, no ice, nothing. To do otherwise is a show of ignorance, a lack of couth. Horsefeathers! Who says?

When cognoscenti, self-proclaimed or otherwise, lay down a rule for taste without any explanation or amplification, the red flag should go up. What is so superior about their taste buds compared to yours other than that theirs have been trained to differentiate one taste from another? NOTHING. For example, by some quirk of nature some people just happen to love cod liver oil! There may not be many, mind you, but they are there. Now, does that make them a bunch of rubes? If somebody wants a Mortlach and ginger ale, fine. They won't be getting the true taste of Mortlach, but it's *their* taste buds - now that's the point.

To the lover of pure malt, then, the following may not only be heresy but blasphemy as well. There is no argument that the mixing of malt Scotch with anything, even water, does modify the taste. There is a difference, however, between adding water and adding some of the other "mixes." Water is pure and is already part of the liquor. Indeed, adding water as a diluent is exactly what was done originally. One must remember that water in Scotland is very soft so that any dilution modifies the original flavour only very slightly for an appreciable reduction in strength. It should be kept in mind that a true tasting will also include the "splash" - remember? To those that do mix, the only heresy is that their taste buds are different and that they will not, indeed cannot, taste the real material. If they can afford to dilute a twenty-five year old Macallan with soda pop - so be it! We will try to restrain our opinions on their taste, or couth - or lack of it.

However, it should be stated again that with any mix, the malt will not taste *anything* like the pure thing - and the title of "purist" cannot be claimed. Not that a "lout" cannot be a connoisseur, *au contraire mon ami.* Here is a case in point.

Not so long ago, if anything but red wine was ordered to accompany warm red-blooded meats, or white wine with seafood and poultry, one was considered an ignoramus, a nincompoop, an omadhaun of the first magnitude. But if that same person does that now, everybody respects him or her for being themselves, for knowing what they like and what they want. One day I went into a local restaurant very well known for its *haute cuisine* and ordered a Dover sole amandine. I love the nuts and the lemon but not the butter. So, I asked for some tartar sauce! I do not know which I enjoyed more, the taste of the fish with the Tartar sauce, or the maître d's attack of apoplexy. Having endured his calling me an ignoramus and a Tartar, I told him it took one to know one and that the next time he served any vinegar-based sauce, to do so in a glass or ceramic dish and not a metal one. I paid my bill, never to return. I do believe the point had been made.

In any weather where sweat has been raised, the Lowland malt is favoured, but not chilled. If chilled, the effect may be even more unusual in that its original lightness makes its ingestion virtually unnoticeable - until it's too late.

Generally speaking then, malt Scotch whisky as an aperitif should be selected following three basic rules, one dealing with the food that follows, the second depending on the activity in which one has engaged, if any, and lastly, the weather or ambient temperature. Before going into details it would be well to review the very general characteristics of the various regions once again, and this time lend a bit more attention to the body. It is the body of the malt Scotch that is in essence the governing factor in that it will in turn influence the aftertaste - the critical element in evaluating malt Scotch.

The Island malts are generally quite easily recognizeable because of the iodoform characteristic. The body is usually heavy with little balance between the smoke and the peat. The latter will definitely "colour" the smoke with the "tint" of iodine. In decreasing order of strength or weight of body there is Ardbeg, Lagavulin,

Laphroig, and Talisker among the better known brands. These are definitely the cold and rainy weather drinks favoured after the trail or following other low-exertion activity in late autumn or winter. Providing the room is not too warm, such a selection can be made and diluted to suit the palate as a complement to any gamey meat. The lighter the main course, the lighter the body, always within the Island "family" of course. Some of the Island malts can be diluted as much as fifty percent without any loss of character or effect with the lightest of the gamey dishes.

When a percentage of dilution is first mentioned, the question invariably arises as to what is meant. The explanation is that, for the fifty percent dilution mentioned above for example, a glass half full with malt Scotch whisky has the other half topped off with water. Rest assured that in the case of the Glenfarclas 105 such a dilution is not exaggerated. By the same token, a twenty-five-percent dilution means that a glass contains seventy-five percent malt Scotch whisky and twenty-five percent water. A ten-percent dilution contains ninety percent malt Scotch and ten percent water. There may be discussion on the matter, but then it would not be improper to quote this book as an authority because "cutting" or diluting malt Scotch for the purposes intended here is not only an uncommon practice, but no other source is known to this writer.

The next category of malt Scotch that is readily recognizeable is the Lowland malt. These are the ones found south of the Greenoch-Dundee line, the imaginary border between the Highlands and the Lowlands. The Lowland malts are generally lighter of body and colour. They have an excellent balance between peat and smoke and need not be diluted more than fifteen percent. Being lighter,they make an ideal, unobtrusive, aperitif.

Other categories are not that easily recognizable except by the geography of their regions. The Strathclyde region is the "hammerhead" configuration at the south end of the Greenoch-Dundee line. The south Strathclyde area was better known as the home of the Campbeltown malts of which only Glen Scotia and Springbank remain. Though a little heavier of body than the Lowland malts, they nevertheless can find their place therewith and, recognizing that many things change with time, this source now classifies these Campbeltowns with the Lowlands. Oban is the northern point of the "hammerhead" and almost a west coast Highland. It has the body of the Highland malt and a touch of the sea, not unlike Dalmore or Clynelish. The west Highland and the east Highland

(Grampian) malts differ from each other in that the west Highland are heavier than the traditional Grampian. The traditional Grampian malts are further divided into two regions: the Speyside along the north-south Elgin-Dufftown line and the east-west Tayside to the south. The western Highland malts might well reach down to encompass all of the Caledonian region and include Oban. The eastern malts are generally mellower and smoother and excellent after dinner drinks — *pousse-cafés par excellence*. The western ones make the better table drinks.

CHAPTER 6
WITH CHEESE PLEASE

Malt Scotch whisky with cheese can be one of the most pleasing experiences that one can have. By pure accident I found that the combination of a Linkwood slightly diluted by a few lumps of melting ice together with some old Canadian strong just slightly sweating was absolutely delightful. The experience was unique and led to some of the most exquisite experiments of my life. A Liederkrantz with Mortlach is another discovery and there are many, many more. Not all of these experiments or "accidents" were that exciting but there were yet others that, by comparison, truly put Champagne and Caviar in the bourgeois category.

Though there are over four hundred different cheeses manufactured around the world, they differ principally in name and shape. Authorities state that there are probably no more than eighteen distinct cheese varieties. This makes it rather cozy in marrying them up with the malts. The cheese lover will recognize the major varieties that follow and on which our analysis has been based. It should be remembered that all of this is still very much a matter of taste and that the general rule of thumb for balancing and enhancing very much applies.

THE NATURE OF CHEESE

Cheeses differ primarily in their moisture content together with the chief microorganism responsible for the ripening. Low moisture (hard) cheeses ripened by bacteria are Cheddar, Romano, Swiss, Edam and Gouda. Medium moisture cheeses (semi-hard) ripened by bacteria are Brick, Muenster and Trappist. Those ripened by mold and bacteria are Roquefort, Gorgonzola and Stilton. High moisture (soft) cheeses ripened by bacteria are Liederkranz and Limburger while Camembert is ripened by mold and bacteria. With the above in mind, it is not difficult now to

Swiss, Liederkranz, Oka and Bel Paese. The range is endless.

classify any of the others known to us such as a Brie, Parmesan, Provolone or Feta. What is indeed more interesting is the variety of taste within each of these "families." All of the above should be considered only as basic background in order to identify the cheese itself and not the taste.

One cheese which can be disposed of rather quickly is processed or "plastic" cheese. Some people do like it and therefore it was tried on salted cheese crackers. Since it is rather bland anyway and does not have any "blending" quality, it needed a malt that would not be overpowering yet stand on its own as smooth and delicate. Unfortunately, this characterless cheese required a top of the medium-priced line of malt Scotch. There was no way that this experiment warranted anything more sophisticated than a Macallan twelve year old or a Balvenie. Sadly, the salty cracker massacred the liquor and, most unfortunately, the cheese could not do without its cracker.

THE TASTE OF CHEESE

Having disposed of this poor orphan, the more traditional cheeses come to mind. The traditionals provide a very wide range of choices and together with the variety of malt Scotch at one's command, the combinations are not only endless, but some are truly exquisite.

Much like the many brands of malt Scotch which are divided into those that are smooth and nutty as compared to those that are smoky or iodoform, there is a similarity with cheeses in that some are sharp while others are either neutral or actually smooth. To this, however, must be added the distinct flavour of some cheeses as compared to others. For example an old strong cheddar is sharp but there is a woody taste to it that makes it quite distinct from other cheddars. In this hard category, most readers who know the basic cheeses will readily recognize the difference between the old strong cheddar and Swiss which is also sharp but with a distinct difference. It will also be recognized that the Edam is much closer to the Swiss than to the old strong cheddar though they are still in the same category. Gouda must be the least sharp of all the hard cheeses. And so it is with the semi-hards and the soft cheeses with which we will deal.

It would now seem appropriate to ask if there are different cheeses for different occasions, or moods, or times of the day, or weather, as in the case of malt Scotch whiskies. The answer is no. Cheese can be a meal in itself. Or again, it is quite acceptable after the hunt (but spare me the sherry!), at the end of a meal, definitely as a snack at the end of an evening or again after a good game of billiards. Now, many will say that tradition would have cheese consumed only with the appropriate wine. So be it, peasants! That is what this book is all about, and this is the first real opportunity to discuss the propriety of malt Scotch with a specific food.

Let us start at the beginning - with a good hard cheese. Unlike malt Scotch, none of which is bad, there may be some cheeses that are either too fresh or too old. They may not have been brought to room temperature or *chambré* as they say in French. In essence, in order to make a good combination, one must be familiar with the cheese that has been chosen, otherwise the experience will not be the best. The first experience will long be remembered. As mentioned before, my first experience was a happenstance, without the benefit of all the rules that have been developed so far. Fortunately, everything was individually at its peak - the Linkwood was sublime and the old Canadian strong cheddar exceptional. It was the result of this chance meeting of all the elements that prompted me to look further and deeper into what is now to me a whole new world of gastronomy.

The appreciation of cheese in combination with malt Scotch can be accomplished in two ways. The first is to take a bite of cheese with or without cracker or crust, masticate, swallow and then take a sip of malt Scotch right away, as if to wash the cheese down. The fumes of both cheese and malt meet somewhere inside and the exhalation is sheer delight. The other way is to take a bite of cheese, again with or without cracker or crust, but this time a sip of malt is taken as the cheese is being masticated. The works are then swallowed. In either case it can only be described as sinfully beautiful. Two things to remember. In the first case, the aftertaste quality of the malt is most important because it virtually has to act on its own. Actually, it doesn't matter too much so long as the combination is right. Secondly, every effort should be made to dispense with the cracker, particularly if it is a soda cracker and salty. It may do something for the cheese but it certainly won't do anything for the malt Scotch. It is said that many tasters take bread with their samples. They do NOT. They eat bread AFTER tasting the sample. Dough is dough and very much a neutralizer. It is said that dough absorbs liquid better and creates a "holding area" that keeps the cheese and malt away from each other till the last minute. An interesting idea, but pure fancy. Though cheese may be a bit much without the company of dough, the dough in all tastings is meant to cleanse or neutralize. When the companion dough is meant as a staple or part of the food, then do ensure its neutrality. If you must eat something with cheese, let it be bread.

Some say that the English bulldog is so ugly that it is a handsome beast. Likewise, old Canadian strong is so sharp and strong as cheeses go that these characteristics are in fact its beauty. Care must be exercised in choosing the accompanying whisky so as to enhance or balance the relationship between the cheese and the whisky properly. On the other hand, the sharpness of Swiss and Edam may be as evident but in a different way and without the strength. It therefore requires a different malt Scotch combination. A little more body is needed but absolutely no peat or smoke. Tullibardine comes to mind, diluted no more than five percent if at all. Now for Gouda. It really needs a little bit of help, but with the right combination it is right there with the rest of them. Because of its flatness, a smooth and mellow Islay (Bunnahabhain) was tried first. The Gouda took off whatever iodine or smoke there was in the liquor and transferred it onto itself, and with the lactate influence - well, what more can be said. Some might want to try a stronger Islay malt and others might feel that Oban has something to offer. Be my guest. That is the beauty of experimenting.

If the next category, the semi-hards, was fun compared to the hards, the soft was hilarious. The reason is that there are so many more of them and the experimenting was so much more "demanding." One of the things that now requires attention is whether the cheese has been ripened by action of bacteria alone or by bacteria and mold. Cheeses ripened by bacteria alone have a tendency to be a bit sharper than those ripened by bacteria and mold. According to cheese experts this is because the mold itself is musty and at some stage that mold "flavours" the bacteria.

With the semi-hard cheeses, the range of flavours is going to be considerably broader, even more so than in the soft cheeses. We must now decide if we want to match or to contrast. In matching a cheese with a malt you are going to take, for instance, a Brick, which is sharp as compared to a Trappist, and match it with a Dalmore, which is a strong-bodied, well-balanced Highland malt. Going to an Islay would overpower the Brick cheese and quite possibly soften the iodine or smoke. This then would be a contrast, but not necessarily a good one. A better contrast, as opposed to a match, would require a milder cheese. This is where the balancing of the cheese and malt is as important as the balance in the malt itself.

In doing both a balance and a contrast with Trappist for example, an Auchriosk is recommended for the balance, whereas a slightly diluted Lochnagar is suggested for the contrast. Roquefort poses an interesting challange. For match or balance there is little doubt that Talisker does a good job. For the contrast, however, a Mortlach might be better because of its "musty" characteristic.

The real fun of "mix and match" begins with semi-hard cheeses possessing flavours that are off the beaten track. Among the better known there are *kirsch, fines herbes*, and *pepper* and the semi-aromatics such as the *Bel Paese*. What now! The answer is - experiment. For example, it was found that a kirsch responded very well to a Balvenie and vice versa. A medium pepper cheese was very well balanced with a Tobermory or a Macallan.

CHAPTER 7
THE MEAT OF THE MATTER

To the extent that malt Scotch whisky can be considered an exotic drink, so also can some meats. One such preparation which suits malt Scotch admirably is Steak Tartar! Ah - the sheer delight of rosy flesh rendered so subtle in liquid velvet can make one wonder at the nature of paradise.

Before getting into this delicacy, however, there is a general rule for enjoying malt Scotch as a table drink with meats. There are many meats of course: beef, lamb, mutton, pork. There are glandular meats such as liver and kidneys. There are combinations of these meats such as steak and kidney pie, and there are yet other combinations with other meats. Really, the possibilities are virtually endless.

How then to give a general rule? The matter becomes somewhat tricky and requires much experimentation. Let us go back once again to the basic tastes associated with malt Scotch. Remember the Island malts with the iodoform characteristic? Hang on to it. Then there is the soft, delicate Lowland malt; the heavier, yet subtle Campbeltown; and wide ranging varieties of the Grampians with their play on balance with slightly lighter body and the delightful aftertaste.

Considering the possible combinations and keeping in mind the small margin for error affecting a suitable match with food, it is not difficult to go wrong. Fortunately, the general rule of keeping the sharps with the sharps and the softs with the softs prevents us from doing so. By the same token it is easy to stay on track with a general, all-purpose drink. The Deanston, diluted about five percent, is highly recommended. This gives enough body without trying to create an accent. Now on the other hand, a Lagavulin, undiluted, with sharp, hot, Steak Tartar is a combination that will never be forgotten.

With a sweeter, more discreet Steak Tartar recipe, you might want to try a Bowmore or Bunnahabhain, undiluted. With Steak Tartar, as with any other meat of character, whether rich or heavy, such as liver, an all-purpose malt Scotch is not recommended. Rather, stay with something strong enough to balance off the meat. What is meant by balancing in this instance is not a matter of addressing the taste by pitting strong against weak, or maintaining an even keel with two weaks or two strongs together. It is a question of combining two flavours that will actually provide a physiological or metabolic balance for the stomach. For example, while Talisker is very much an Island malt, it does not have the right weight for the hot, sharp variety of Steak Tartar but would do much better with the sweeter one. Talisker, on the other hand, is excellent with liver. Lagavulin is not.

For those who like things that are off the beaten track, Steak Tartar can be quite an experience in the kingdom of malts. If not the sovereign, it is at least a very princely offering. After observing a number of maîtres d' producing all sorts of combinations that were supposed to be standard, or not asking me for my spicing preferences, there was no doubt left in my mind that personal experimenting was necessary. It became a very serious part of my research and as a result, four basic recipes have been developed in response to four basic tastes.

These tastes can be either sharp and hot or smooth and mild or a combination thereof. While some might prefer the latter, it should be remembered that any Steak Tartar is already rich and heavy and to have it any richer might be just a bit too much.

The basic ingredients remain the same: meat, anchovies, capers, olive oil, vinegar, mustard, garlic and the yolk of an egg. Select only the best and leanest ground beef. The filet is excellent. To mix the ingredients, a wooden bowl is preferable. Start with the anchovies, which should be crushed to a true paste with a bit of olive oil. Next come the onions and the first of the variables. Red spanish onions contribute to a smooth taste as opposed to white onions which provide a sharp taste. In either case, the onion, about the size of a golf ball per six ounces of meat, should be chopped very fine and then mashed into the anchovy paste. Add about eight capers and also mash into the paste. Next add about two tablespoons of vinegar, the second variable. White vinegar contributes to the sharp taste whereas wine or red vinegar contributes to the smooth variety. To this concoction, add some garlic. Some individuals prefer simply to rub the mixing bowl with a garlic clove at the very beginning. That is a bit too subtle and it is preferable to crush a clove the size of half a thimble and mash it into the paste. Another ingredient is added at this time, the mustard. The smooth taste requires a good Dijon mustard, while the sharp strong taste calls for a powdered mustard such as Keen's. About one teaspoon should do the trick. Now for the meat. Dump the whole six ounces into the bowl and macerate. A true Steak Tartar should be like a paste and it is not a matter of the four or five minutes most maîtres d' will take at your table. The back of a soup spoon is an excellent macerator and the process usually takes a solid fifteen minutes. To this paste, the last variable is now added: the pepper. While black pepper is not as strong as white pepper, be cautioned not to use more than a quarter of a teaspoon. Any more can kill this delightful creation. Again macerate to ensure even distribution, not only of the pepper but of all the other ingredients with the meat. Then add the last ingredient, the egg yolk, and macerate some more. This makes the whole thing hang together and gives a true paste consistency. And *voilà - le Steak Tartar "à la Bernard."*

Many prefer the strong and smooth variety with the white onions, the powdered mustard, the wine vinegar and the black pepper. Any excess smoothness is balanced off with a good, virgin Bunnahabhain or a Laphroig with a few drops of water. Ahhhhhhh!

Why this recipe? Well, it should give the reader a better idea of the exotic possibilities and make it easier to select the malt to match the meat. The strong hot Tartar would require a Lagavulin to effect a good balance.

Going on along the same lines, venison is not too far removed from the above and whether broiled or prepared some other way, a heavy Campbeltown malt or something like the Clynelish or Dalmore would be excellent.

Now for roast of beef and some of the "lesser" concoctions. For those preparations, nobody can go wrong following the formula first mentioned above. Keep in mind that the fatty meats should be well cut by a fuller-bodied malt Scotch than a Lowlander.

Of all the meats, beef is probably the best known for the variety of preparations it offers. Corned beef is a prime example. It is intricate to prepare but the selection of the accompanying drink is easy.

Meat varations are endless.

Other preparations such as Swiss steak, Hamburg steak, braised beef, beef hash and so on, deserve consideration as well. Unless spice and *friture* come into play, they all have much the same basic taste and the best we can do is go for a neutral type of malt Scotch - such as a good Lowland. The strength should be varied according to mood. There are two other beef preparations that that are worthy of special mention. The first is filet mignon wrapped in bacon and smothered with onions and mushrooms. To complement this preparation consider a rich mustard sauce. Strangely enough, the beef comes through and here the

Glendronach aged in sherry casks deserves a tip of the hat. The other preparation is a black pepper steak. Because of the cut of the meat usually used, which is a bit on the bland side, the pepper does come out but a Dalmore will more than handle it.

Finally, something must be said about the roast - say a standing rib! Unfortunately, powdered English mustard or horseradish will not let much flavour come through, and what is left should not be obliterated by the malt Scotch. Now the Cragganmore needs no enhancing and it can stand so well on its own that it is a natural. It is so well matched that anything hidden from within will invariably come out.

From beef, we can progress to the younger fellow, veal. No matter how prepared, this is a delicate, fine-grained and velvety meat that calls for a light-bodied malt Scotch in the Deanston or Springbank category. If it is delicately spiced, or even spiced at all, a slightly watered-down Balvenie is suggested in spite of the sacrilegious nature of that act. In this case forgiveness should not be too difficult to come by.

Veal is somewhat like lamb in the variety of its preparations. There are some specialties like curry and schnitzel that might be considered, but then this introduces foreign preparations, which is not intended at this time. It would be preferable to stay with the dishes of the areas most associated with malt Scotch.

Lamb! Can it really be called that, or is it mutton? Remember what was said about the fatty meats! In this case consider selecting a sharp, full- bodied liquor such as a Glenallachie. Talisker might be a pleasant surprise. One of the things that must be remembered is that lamb, in many instances, may carry a woolly taste to it, unless great care is exercised in its preparation. It is to be noted that the Bretons and the Scots make very good use of onions and garlic in preparing this meat, whether it be roast or casserole. Inasmuch as this does have the effect of offsetting the fatty taste, one only has to remember that, though it may be an acquired taste, the combination of lamb and the Greek wine retsina should give a hint as to what to expect. Some will automatically cough at even the thought of Retsina with its resinous taste, but then what can be said about Ardbeg and iodine! Generally speaking, lamb will call for a rather full-bodied malt, preferably unbalanced so that either the smoke or the peat can come through and balance the wool. This is not a meat that can be enhanced too well. Although it might be done if virtually all the fat is trimmed off, a really good amount of seasoning is added plus a long, low heat in the company of "stewage."

Carrying on with lamb, other than the roast and casserole preparations, there are different cuts such as chops which quite naturally will carry a little less fat. In such cases a lighter type of malt makes for a rather pleasant combination. But, lamb being lamb, my own preference is to stay with the Lowland malts that have more body, adding a little bit more water - but not more than a few drops - in order to up the flavour. Lamb can also be barbecued, curried, stewed and stuffed. In all cases it is a question of considering the strength and weight of the food and selecting a drink to balance it. Do not try to enhance lamb. Only the Greeks with their retsina can do a significant job. Rather, enjoy a well-balanced meal - that is what the dietitians say!

And now for rabbits, hares and squirrels. It is strongly recommended that wild rabbit be avoided. On the other hand, there is little controversy about hare. It is suggested that neither hare nor rabbit be drawn before hanging as they may become musty. If they do though, there is an appropriate remedy - an equally musty malt, like Mortlach! These small four-footers are quite tender and delicately flavoured, in which case we should also go for a delicately flavoured malt in order to effect a proper balance. A Balvenie comes to mind. Should you want to enhance these meats, select a weak Springbank but if you wish to taste the liquor without obliterating the meat, then a Tomatin would be good. Whether fried, roasted or in casserole, the meat will not be that much different and the above suggestions should hold.

Then there is our fat, flat-snouted friend, the porker. What can we say about pork? Quite a bit actually. Ah, what delectable dishes can be conjured up from the anatomy of this animal. Tenderloin. Although it can be prepared in a number of ways, there will always be a basic taste with the same characteristics: a taste not unlike chicken. A stuffed tenderloin is more moist and the spice of the stuffing may well be imparted to the meat itself so that we are looking at a balancing situation. The same cannot be said of pork chops, particularly when prepared in a batter. In this case, a light Lowland malt like the Deanston is recommended - or again, something musty like Mortlach or Littlemill.

And what about ham? A fellow well-met with quite a bit to offer. The meat is basic and traditionally salty due largely to the smoking. This meat sets up probably the most challenging situation because invariably it is covered with a sweet and/or spicy glazing. The decision has to be made whether to enhance the meat or have the meat enhance the liquor. Because of its naturally strong taste, it is difficult to enhance this meat, particularly if the glazing is sweet. A gentle Island malt like Bunnahabhain or Bowmore gives excellent results. These will blend in nicely with the sweetness of the glazing, and the meat brings out the smoke. Insofar as the spicy glazing is concerned, both the meat and the spice are sufficiently strong that neither the whisky nor the ham can do anything for each other. In such cases, select the most gentle of all the Lowlands and use it as an *ordinaire*.

Virtually all the meats that can go into our diets can go equally well with something else in combinations such as casseroles, loaves, stews, steak and kidney pies, and other interesting dishes. These will be dealt with in the chapter on potpourri , but in closing this one, I would like to offer a few a few words about glandular meats such as liver and kidneys. These tend to be stronger than average meats and should be balanced with a malt Scotch a bit fuller than usual. However, because such meats are not really sharp unless improperly cooked, the malt should also be slightly on the mellow side and a Bowmore or a Tobermory is highly recommended.

The general rule above is just that - general, and very general at that. Sweetbreads, heart and tongue are a bit milder and brains quite so. For heart and tongue, the variety of preparations is broader than for sweetbreads and brain. For these meat specialties it is very much a case of bringing out the best in the malt Scotch whisky. For sweetbreads and brain, you want to cut the sweetness out and use that route to bring out the best in the liquor but not by overpowering the dish. A Knockando or Inchgower would do very nicely. Heart, on the other hand, is very much like kidney and the added sharpness justifies the brands in the paragraph above.

There is a virtual wealth of meat dishes that fall neither into the traditional roast or potpourri categories, nor are they identified by their sauces. Rather, they are known by their preparation and presentations. In this category we find Beef Stroganoff, Burgundian, à *la Normandie* and *Mironton*, to name but a few. How are these to be handled? With great care. Particularly where the preparation involves the use of wines (not in the sauce but in the preparation, such as *flambé)*. Fortunately, malt Scotch whisky will blend in rather well. The trick here is to identify the predominant

By all means try your own accents —— but cautiously.
(Courtesy Toshiba Canada.)

characteristic and then determine if you want to balance or enhance. Usually such preparations are on the smooth side.

Are there more meats? Of course there are, and it would be no trouble to write an entire encyclopaedia suggesting a particular malt for each individual preparation. It is you that should now meet the challenge through experimentation. You can only be the winner, particularly when you make a discovery that is all yours. You can be a winner in another way also. It would be interesting to come out with a number of very specific combinations in some future edition of this book. If you would like to join me, send in some comments about your experiments and experiences. There's a challenge for you!

CHAPTER 8
ON THE WING

What a foul thing to think that fowl and whisky don't have a pecking order. Of course they do, and a good one! Because of the exotic reputation of malt Scotch, first thoughts might well turn to equally exotic preparations for fowl such as Pheasant under Glass or Peking Duck or *Canard à l'orange*. Indeed, these dishes do have their place alongside malt Scotch whisky, in the same manner as Steak Tartar. But being a little on the exotic side, it is understandable that more realistic thoughts would turn to the good old roast chicken or turkey as the traditional bird dish. Insofar as drink is concerned, it is difficult to associate such dishes with anything else than white wine. On this point, no argument. Chicken and turkey by themselves are a very creditable challenge being a weak lot. But as stated before, malt Scotch can take up many challenges. Indeed, there is a very pleasant surprise awaiting anyone turning once again to our trusty old Deanston. But a suggestion - the flesh is so weak that the malt Scotch should be diluted at least fifteen percent.

It is much more usual to find chicken and turkey as part of another dish or as a combination along with spices and vegetables. In those instances, such as in the case of birds with more character, malt Scotch again comes into its own.

The range of tastes offered by bird flesh is wide enough to require, indeed demand, considerable care in the selection of malts to accompany these dishes because any differences, wide as the range of taste may be, are very subtle. Consequently, it is important to balance or enhance in such a manner as to avoid any possibility of rendering the whole dish bland. Keeping in mind that enhancing a weak dish is virtually impossible, the exercise becomes one of balancing. In the case of weak dishes, this is quite a trick because two opposites can balance as in the case of +2 and -2. They end up as 0. If the flesh is weak there isn't A+ or A-.

The balance must therefore be a match of two weaks or two strongs. For example, pheasant requires at least a Clynelish or a Bowmore - chicken, a Deanston.

On this basis, let us go ahead and consider our friends the chicken and the turkey. Roast chicken is not something that can be enhanced too easily. On the other hand it might just serve as the enhancer to the malt Scotch that would otherwise be looked upon as "one of many." In this case the malt Scotch should not have too much body but, nor should it be too well-balanced. Mortlach is the first that comes to mind but better yet would be something with a bit more of the smooth smoke. Even traces of peat should be avoided because peat is dry and so is chicken. The result is a bland combination but Tobermory, Ben Wyvis or Inchgower, each in their own way, would be enhanced most effectively by chicken and provide a pleasant experience.

More often than not, roast chicken will not have much seasoning if at all. Savory in the stuffing is the old standby and some will add thyme. It is very difficult to season chicken itself. That is probably the reason why a sauce chef can have a field day with it and therein lies the importance of knowing the makeup of the sauce. As nature would have it, the characteristics of savory are such that it can only enhance whatever light malt Scotch is selected. One reason is that savory itself has a smoky characteristic. Other methods of preparing chicken range from fondues, batters and fries to the highly spiced oriental dishes. In such cases, most gourmets would recommend that nothing be taken with the dish, but to relish the dish itself for all it is worth. No argument here either, and it is suggested that in such cases a malt Scotch that has a very staying aftertaste should be selected: almost a liqueur quality such as a Macallan. Should such quality be relegated to the dining table? Well...some gastronomes spend more on the liquid than on the solids...so!

In all of this, little has been said about the difference between the light and the dark meat. That difference is an appreciable one and not to be disregarded. In many instances, hosts will recognize that some prefer white to dark and vice versa. It should be noted that all of the foregoing was directed towards the light meat. Dark meat is a bit juicier and its taste is not as fowl-like. Alas, as in the case of the white meat, the dark meat also has little power to enhance the malt Scotch. It is therefore necessary to have a malt that will stand alone, in the medium range of the Campbeltowns - a Cardhu for example.

And now for the chicken's country cousin - the turkey - the very symbol of Thanksgiving and Christmas. Actually, all that has been said about chicken can also be said about turkey - and in spades. The only difference is that turkey, being a little bit tougher by nature, winds up by being scientifically "moisturized" so that in the final analysis, any difference is so small that just about all the malts selected for chicken would do as well with turkey.

In the land of the Celts, from south Brittany to the Orkneys, the winged wonder *par excellence* is the goose. Here the brown and white meat is richer with much less of a contrast one from the other than with chicken or turkey. It *demands* a well-balanced and stronger malt Scotch than our two former fine-feathered friends. A Tamdhu or Tomatin seems to have just the right stuff to do a proper balancing act. This bird is too strong to go into the enhancement category. But one must be careful of what surrounds the roast goose. One must never forget one of the principal rules stated at the very beginning of this work when discussing the merits of malt Scotch as an aperitif. Always take into consideration what comes before, after or with the entree, nay - the entire meal. In the case of the goose, the rich characteristic of the meat makes the choice of the right malt all the more important.

Next in line must be the duck. This beaky baby is prepared in more ways than the number of stops on its migratory journey. By the same token, there will be an equal number of malt Scotch whiskies to keep it company. *Canard à l'orange* is a real challenge because it can be both something for balancing and something for enhancing. Because of the trouble that goes into its preparation, it should be taken as a balancing challenge and a Balvenie is recommended. With a suprème de canard we are looking at a roast combination with wild rice, and what could be better than any number of the medium Grampians slightly diluted? For example, a Milton-Duff or a Dufftown-Glenlivet would be excellent. Considering the possible number of recipes that remain, it might be best to go on to another bird lest this be turned into a cook book. The important thing to remember, particularly in the case of duck, is that the choice must be made either to balance or to enhance. No matter which way you look at it, duck is duck and a slight fishy flavour may very well creep in. So, over and above the expensive suggestions that have been made, keep in mind the lighter Islay malts. There is a surprise in there for you.

Partridge. This fine feathered friend can be quite gamey and so presents, once again, a balancing proposition. There are not altogether too many ways of preparing partridge, so we are not faced with a wide choice of malt Scotch whiskies. It is regarded as a white meat bird and therefore a bit on the dry side. As such it must be thoroughly cooked and "larded." It will also require something to cut the grease as well as moisten without overpowering. Although there is nothing more regrettable than diluting a well-balanced and full-bodied liquor, that is what is required here. Dalmore immediately comes to mind. If your pocketbook can take it, your palate will be forever grateful.

What have we left? Delightful little things, that's what: guinea-fowl, pea-fowl, pheasant, quail, grouse, squab, and pigeon. If you think of any others, do write in and, fear not, we shall do them justice.

Guinea-fowl is not as tough as pea-fowl but both definitely need larding. Insofar as these two species are concerned, bird meat is bird meat is bird meat. The best thing to do with these is to use them in fricassees and pies, or mix them up into a potpourri. Even in the potpourri, their flavour is there and a good selection of malt Scotch would be something like Fettercairn or Linkwood.

It would be appropriate to step aside here for a minute and point out that the preparation of fowl is similar to that of fish, not for the end result but in the manner of preparation. Fowl, like fish, can be roasted, panned, fried, fricasseed, broiled, braised, planked. It can also be prepared with any number of spices, like curry, while sauces may utilize the giblets. Ah - the giblets. Something absolutely delectable, particularly the liver and the heart. These fall into the category of glandular meats, however, and you might wish to go back to the meats in the previous chapter to check the comments made at that time. In any case, glandular meats from fowl are indeed a treat and can very easily make up a dish of their own. On the other hand they can add considerably to any potpourri. All that needs to be said at this time in matching up the proper malt with any of these preparations is that the taste of the dish should be thoroughly familiar and only then should the decision be made whether to balance or enhance.

Pheasant has a lot going for it, but one should not go overboard for what may be just presentation. For example, pheasant under glass is just another term for a broiled bird. With wild rice, it is indeed difficult to beat - but it is still just a broiled bird. Pheasant is also considered to be a white-meat fowl and somewhat on the dry side, though not as much so as the partridge. It is not as gamey and, like canard à l'orange, can easily take up the flavour of its milieu. In this case the preperation with wild rice is excellent in that wild rice has a strong sweetness to it mixed in with a touch of mustiness. Mortlach comes back to mind very easily, but experimenting with a strong Lowland should prove interesting as would the exact opposite such as Highland Park.

Quail is yet another white meat fowl that is nevertheless tender, more so than the others. Though tender, it is not juicy and requires larding, but to a lesser extent than the other white meat fowl. Basted with oil and wrapped in foil, it produces a king's delight. The Littlemill marries very well with quail.

Grouse is a rather dry bird and larding is a must. In a number of areas grouse is a very popular game bird which, come autumn, finds itself on the table in any number of presentations. To overcome the dryness, the oil and foil trick that does wonders to dry meats works well with birds also. Like the guinea fowl, grouse has a tendency to be tough, which makes the addition of moisture a must. Because of this, every attempt is made to avoid the heavy-bodied malts. Heavy meals make great demands on the stomach. Why add to the problem by having an equally heavy-bodied malt? However, this particular bird, like a Welsh rarebit, provides excellence at both ends of the scale. Grouse in the cool of autumn with Dalmore or Clynelish can be sumptuous. But that combination in mid summer would be the opposite. The "official" preference would be for our old friends Deanston and Rosebank. That combination is good at any time.

Where pigeons are concerned, the passenger pigeon that disappeared in the early 1900s was the *pièce de résistance*. What you can find now is only so-so, and is probably best when used in a potpourri. The feathered inhabitants of the city square are a definite no-no because of both law and health.

Squab is best broiled. Because of the size, most cook books refer to the breast being flattened, broiled, buttered and served on toast. No doubt you sense my lack of enthusiasm, but in all fairness to the little beggars, they are good — perhaps as a snack. Pick any light Grampian for this "dish."

Today's menus are so traditionally oriented towards chicken and turkey that we seldom even try any of the lesser known fowl - unless the cook is very enterprising. Nowadays, who but the professional chef, male or female, has the time! A word to the wise, though. When they are well prepared and accompanied by the proper malt Scotch whisky, these potentially bland dishes will surprise even the most blasé of gourmets.

CHAPTER 9
SEA WHAT WE HAVE HERE

The sea, the sea, the wonderful sea. And indeed what wonders it brings to our table. Something to match the wonders of the pot still. Here we have something of a very pleasant and easy task because, with only a few exceptions, we are looking at balancing the iodoform with the very distinctive odor and taste of sea food.

These dishes can be surprisingly well accommodated by even a modest malt Scotch whisky cellar and can produce some very interesting creations. One such creation comes from the use of whisky in the preparation. In Chapter 4 we noted that the true aroma or flavour of the whisky does not come through into the cooking, simply because of the amount of grain alcohol in the blends. In some cases, however, the grain alcohol will fail to mask the stronger aromas in some brands resulting in a rather rough drink. You will never, never, have the delicate smoothness of the pure malt in the blends. But then again, sometimes in cooking, the roughness of the smoke is precisely what is required, what may be necessary to give some character to an otherwise bland sauce, for example. Lemon can only go so far. Whisky can go farther.

The sea produces a wide range of species that can be grouped into two major categories: fish and crustaceans. Some might argue that oysters, clams and mussels are different from each other and different again from the crustaceans such as lobsters and crabs. Rather than be called crustaceans, meaning shellfish, they will all be called precisely that, - shellfish - which will still put them in a class apart from the ordinary fish. That is what the College of Home Economics of Cornell University does, also counting frogs, terrapin and turtles in with shellfish.

Within the fish group there is white fish with less than two percent fat, such as smelt, flounder, perch, pike, pickerel, bass, cod and haddock. Medium fat fish have two percent to five percent fat and include brook trout, mullet and white perch. Fat or oily fish contain five percent or more fat and include salmon, chad, herring, lake trout, bluefish, mackerel and eels. It is important to be aware of these three subgroups because the fat content will bear considerably on the selection of the most appropriate brand of malt Scotch.

Though it is our intent to discuss separately each fish noted above, and others, there are two rules of thumb that apply to fish. Firstly, the oilier or fatter the fish, the less you dilute your brand, and secondly, the oilier or fatter the fish, the fuller the body of the brand must be. In essence, haddock and Tobermory marry very well as would smoked herring and Laphroig.

Once again the decision must be made whether it is better to enhance or to balance. The white and medium fish, with the exception of smelt, are difficult to enhance. On the other hand, these dishes have sufficient character so that they can do a bit of enhancing of their own, and this is where the individuality of both the malt Scotch and the food comes into play. The oily or fat fish are the only ones with which one can experiment, and much like strong meat or fowl, there is yet again the choice of balancing or enhancing.

Shellfish are not necessarily strong, but they have a very distinct character. Prawns and shrimp, if well prepared, have a distinctly sweet and very pleasant taste. Unfortunately, more often than not, restaurant procedures and freezing techniques tend to leave them on the bland side. If one is not careful, lobster can also lose quite a bit of flavour in the preparation. The taste of oysters and clams, when smoked or left in their own juices, can change considerably between acquisition by the chef and presentation at the table. To be enjoyed, the taste of the food should at least resemble that which is anticipated. Crayfish and crabs lean towards the sweet side of lobster. The sweetest meats of all are to be found in frogs, terrapin and turtles.

As there are many ways to prepare meats, so there are also as many ways to prepare fish. You can smoke, fry, boil, broil, simmer, steam, pickle, poach, sauté and cream a fish. It is not necessary to discuss every fish in each preparation above. All the necessary suggestions will be conveyed quite adequately even if we stick to the most popular preparations following the basic principles already laid down. Your own further experimentation will lead you to your own Nirvana.

A delightful dish of shrimps. (Courtesy Toshiba Canada.)

Before moving on to fish dish presentations, one other marine delicacy must be mentioned - roe!!! Just as one might well ask how something so foul smelling as whisky mash can turn out to be so heavenly, so might one ask how the rotten eggs of a sturgeon can be a gourmet's delight. Could this be caviar? Ahhh - Caviar and Champagne! Well try caviar and chilled Bowmore. Laddie, laddie, laddie! Ha ye e'er let the likes grace your gullet? Nae mon, ne'er.

And now for the smelts. There are, of course, many kinds of smelt but the target here is the overgrown river sardine - the one that's the size of a small trout. Deep fried in a cracker batter it is absolutely delicious and moist with a sweet taste and just a touch of fishiness to it. To balance this fish, select a Bunnahabhain diluted ten percent and to enhance, go for a Tobermory also diluted ten percent.

Flounder is a nice white fish that could be grouped with cod and haddock, though flounder, like sole, is a flat fish. The main difference is in the "sectioning" of the flesh. The taste is sufficiently similar for both flounder and sole to be either enhanced or balanced with the same brand of malt Scotch. The Littlemill at ten percent dilution balances very well and a Springbank diluted five percent will both enhance and be enhanced. The amandine preparation would be a standard here. Remember, the preparations discussed here are either the ones which are best known or those that have been found particularly pleasant and satisfying, and the choices may well not be your favourites.

Pickerel, perch, pike and bass are grouped together here for the same reason as flounder and sole. This group is particularly bony and it may be the reason for the somewhat flaky dryness of the flesh. Remember that fish fried will taste different from fish baked. Steaming is my preference because the fish falls apart. After a couple of tries for a good matching brand the Isle of Jura came to mind but unfortunately my initial reaction to a straight-up serving or even a five percent dilution was not impressive. At fifteen percent dilution it was a bit weak but very good and subtle. Dalwhinnie cut about five percent was next. The results were virtually the same. No attempt was made with any Islay because it is certain that they would have overpowered these fish or would have to have been so diluted as to lose character.

The medium fish that follow are similar to the first group of whites after the smelts - insofar as taste is concerned. Most cooks will avoid the amandine preparation with such fish. Go for a fried one for trout, broiled for the mullet and white perch. Littlemill and Springbank are hard to beat with these offerings.

The fat and oily category probably offers the most fun. Unlike the traditional situation where more fun is bad, in this instance more fun is healthy. For example, there is only a bit less iodine here than found in shellfish and we have plenty of vitamins.

Salmon, particularly smoked, is sheer heaven with a slightly diluted Talisker. In the case of smoked salmon, Talisker is diluted ever so slightly, as it is for kipper or smoked herring. Talisker should

Scottish smoked salmon — an experience with few peers.

be more diluted as the salmon becomes more bland through various preparations until we reach a virtually tasteless poached salmon in white sauce. With such bland preparations, a chef usually jumps in with any number of ideas for spices and herbs. This is where your own imagination comes into play in matching it to the proper brand of malt Scotch.

Chad, char, lake trout, and bluefish. My preferred preparation for these specimens is fried or simmered. When fried, the flavour is locked in, but when simmered, there may be a loss of that flavour. However, the flesh is gorgeous. The latter, like bland salmon, allows for spicing and if kept within the bounds of propriety will always make for a sweet, clean taste. Ardbeg, reduced the usual five to ten percent, will invariably do a good job of both balancing and enhancing with these species but expect the unexpected when they are matched with Highland Park.

Eels! My devotion to duty has its limits. I have yet to even taste these beasties. Mindful that any preacher has an obligation to try everything in order to speak from knowledge, you must be made aware that this is one species where you and you alone must be the judge. If you like eels, congratulations and let me know how you make out. Just remember the rules of tasting. You should do quite well.

Shellfish are even more interesting than the oily fish. Particularly in the case of *Escargots à la Bourguignonne*. Of course, the garlic butter is what you really have to contend with here but what fun it is to cut it down with pure Ardbeg or a slightly diluted Laphroig.

Oysters raw and on ice are a real pleasure. Though heavy in cholesterol, they are quite light to the taste with a slightly musty flavour. Surprisingly, a chilled Mortlach produced an excellent result. With raw clams a switch was made to a chilled Highland Park. In both cases it was extremely difficult to enhance, as it was to balance. Neither oysters nor clams change much in soup or cream, and surprisingly, neither does the combination of malt Scotch. When the oysters are smoked, however, they become very heavy and the malt Scotch should be cut down or left unchilled accordingly. If the smoke flavour is pronounced, then a Lagavulin should be considered - and slightly diluted.

Mussels were found to be rather bland. In this case Cragganmore is recommended reduced ten percent for all recipes. This is definitely a time where the food is used principally to bring out or enhance the drink.

Lobster, in my book, comes three ways: à *la Newburg,* cold or just out of the kettle. My overall preference is the cold version. The creamy preparation of the Newburg is definitely a job for Highland Park as is. For the boiled preparation, hot or cold, it would be difficult to improve on Clynelish or Dalmore. Both should be served chilled with the cold lobster, and *au naturel* with the ones coming out of the kettle.

Crab is delightful: in some ways more so than lobster. Isle of Jura is excellent with this creepy crawler, whether hot or cold. Craw and crayfish also fit into this category. In the case of the remaining three critters on our list (the frog, the terrapin and the turtle), one has to choose something equally as delicate as the meat they produce. Rosebank and Glengoyne, slightly diluted, are my choices.

One could go on and on but then there would be no room left for you to experiment. There is enough material here to satisfy just about any palate and those that are even more discriminating will find absolute ecstasy in discovering something different - something new. Enjoy!

CHAPTER 10
A POTPOURRI

The Scots and all the other Celts would have my head for putting such dishes as Cipaille and stews in the same category as haggis and calling it "potpourri." My intention here, however, is to deal with as many dishes as possible that are not specifically meat, fish or fowl.

The first should be haggis if only because of its designation by Robbie Burns as "great chieftain of the puddin' race." Haggis! A maligned delicacy which, indeed, can be a total disgrace if ill prepared, but a true repast if done up properly. Also by tradition it is maintained that there is nothing to beat the combination of Cardhu and Haggis, and there are no arguments on that count from this corner.

But that is not the end of it. Altogether too many folks get the wrong idea about haggis and in so doing also get the wrong idea about other dishes that at first glance might seem repugnant.No doubt that blood or black pudding definitely does not convey the same image as apple pie or strawberry shortcake. Similarly "cooked in a sheep's stomach" does not sound the same as "slowly baked and basted in its own juices." No matter the euphonics. It is the taste that counts and a potpourri has much to offer. Even more when malt Scotch is involved.

As the name implies, this chapter deals with all other dishes that are a bit out of the ordinary or "thrown" together - like stew. Make no mistake, some of these dishes are not only excellent, or can be made so by a good chef, but they can be demanding in their preparation.

Since oats are widely used as a cereal and in other dishes (like haggis) in Scotland and many other parts of the world, this seems to be a good place to start. Oats are among the healthier of foods and are abundant in Scotland. However, they are dry, dry, dry.

Dr. R. Benzie, member of An Quaich, addressing the haggis.

Rolled oats or porridge invariably tastes better if wetted down with milk or cream and flavoured with a good dose of brown sugar. Then again, there is absolutely nothing wrong with lacing the dish. As a matter of fact, if you are on holidays and want to try something different, adding a few drops in the porridge along with the brown sugar brings a totally different aspect to the mealy mush. On a cold morn the really brave soul will substitute the morning "cuppa" with a light, slightly warm Grampian diluted sixty percent with water (of the softest kind - mind you). Needless to say that the morning "grog" is a long standing tradition that need not be reserved to sailors only.

From rolled oats or porridge, let's go to haggis. All Scots, and all Celts for that matter, live by the motto "waste not, want not" and utilize everything from their spartan natural environment. And so it is with haggis. there is meat in that dish - lots of meat, such as liver, heart, kidneys and all the other glandular meats enjoyed in other preparations, and of course, tongue (as in cold braised tongue for the hot summer days). However, lungs and brains admittedly raise a question in many minds. But the taste of these organs is sweet and rich, and adds moisture to the mixture. Furthermore, they are totally delectable - and totally undetectable.

Now, just throwing all these items together is artless and the taste might well be questionable. That is why the ingenious Scottish domestic engineer decided to use rolled oats as a catalyst and add spices to balance and enhance, knowing full well that any added moisture required could be provided by the best drink of all, malt Scotch. The last thing to turn people off is that it is cooked in a sheep's stomach. Believe it. The sheep is dead. The stomach lining has been cleaned out, washed, scoured, everything short of bleached. The stomach is strong, flexible, non-porous: an excellent receptacle and temperature conductor. Hey! Dump the whole thing in, tie it up and put it into a pot of boiling water. That, my friends, is the equivalent of steam cooking. Well prepared, haggis is a good substantial dish whose equal is hard to find. As a drink to go along with that, you are already aware that Cardhu is most difficult to beat. However, there are others, and any of the heavier Lowlands will do the trick. Southern Grampians are also well received. What we are looking for here is something light but with a little more body and a particularly good, equally light, aftertaste.

Cipaille is a French term for a particular type of dish that is half way between shepherd's pie and beef stew. The story goes that it is an old Acadian dish, originating in Brittany. The name comes from the English words "sea" and "pie." Put them together and you have the perfect pronounciation, with the exception that the accent is on the last word. A better sense of pronounciation is given if we use the Spanish si. As in shepherd's pie, there are a lot of potatoes along with an equally generous amount of meat in a meat Cipaille. It can also be made with fish. It is advisable to know the dish in order to match up the malt Scotch, but the description that follows will be brief inasmuch as this is not intended as a cook book.

In both cases the base of the pot, preferably crockery, is lined with potatoes in slices as if they were to be scalloped. Then there is a layer of meat. This can be hare, rabbit, or a mixture of both.

Throw in a pigeon or a few squabs. The idea is to use what you have. Spread another layer of potatoes, then another layer of meat, and so on. In between each layer, paint the potatoes with butter or cream or even milk - so long as the mixture is moist. Top off with potatoes and dry bread crumbs and put it into the oven. Don't forget the spices - the usual ones - and others according to the palate and the imagination.

It would be nice to keep all the meats for meat Cipaille, birds for a bird Cipaille and fish for the fish Cipaille. In this case, shellfish does not have its place. Cipaille is strictly for the white, medium oily fish. Instead of all potatoes, rolled oats can be nicely substituted. The trick is that the dish should not become too dry. Whether it does or not, there is another very important element - what to drink with the meal!

The choice is not difficult. With the meats, something a bit heavier than Cardhu is recommended, say a Knockando. A bit on the expensive side, but diluted twenty percent, it is nothing short of marvelous. A fish Cipaille requires a good Bowmore or Bunnahabhain. Tobermory is fine but a little bit on the rich side. A bird Cipaille calls for our old friends, Deanston or Rosebank - something fresh and light.

Now that we are into the pies, our potpourri becomes extensive with just about anything that can go into a pie: steak and kidney, pigeon, straight meat, shepherd's, and the list goes on.

Steak and kidney is a classic which combines steak, a rather bland meat, with kidneys, which have a distinctive character. Kidneys should not be strong to the taste. If they are, they have not been properly cleaned and the dish should be sent back. Most preparations will give the impression of something dry, thick and pasty. That calls for something just a bit lighter than Dalmore or Clynelish yet with as much character. Few, if any, are better than Glenmorangie. Again, this means diluting a masterpiece, but then, is not every malt Scotch whisky a masterpiece?

Shepherd's pie is very much like Cipaille with the exception that there are not the layers of meat and potatoes. Of course, in some variations of the shepherd's pie, there are no potatoes and this is just a regular meat pie with the cook not really knowing the difference. A shepherd's pie must have potatoes. Ask the Irish! This is generally quite moist on its own because of the fat in the meat.

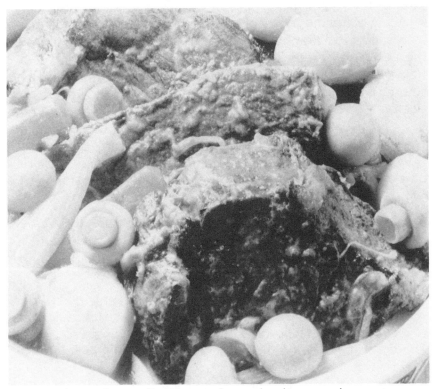

Potpourris can be as distinct as the malts that are chosen to accompany them. (Courtesy Toshiba Canada.)

Glenesk is a good brand for this dish as would be Linkwood or a slightly more diluted Cragganmore.

Insofar as the other pies are concerned (and there are many, the range being limited only by the imagination of the cook), it is best to go with a rule of thumb. Where pies are concerned, remember the crust - in itself a typically mealy, pasty substance. However, it is usually light. (If you have a heavy, greasy crust, change the cook!) Be that as it may, the crust should be kept in mind when thinking of the substance of the dish. Remember the original rule of thumb based on the enhancing or balancing principle. If the dish is light, more than likely a light malt to enhance, or a heavier to balance. Heavy/sharp for a rich dish, heavy/smooth for a bland dish. The same applies to pies.

Now a little bit about the pots and stews. Here also there is a wide variety of flavours again limited only .by the imagination of the cook. However, where pies will usually be "blanded" by the pastry, stews with their vegetables, onions, and spicing can be anything but bland. Think of the French ragoût! The rule of thumb in this instance does not hold very well because the variations on the stew theme are so broad: hot, sharp, bland, smooth, rich, lean, heavy, light... The overall champion has to be Deanston, with its strength varied according to the job it has to do. However, let us not forget that we have so far really taken only beef into consideration and we have not said anything about stews based on lamb, veal, pork or combinations thereof. Lamb requires special consideration in light of what was said in the meat chapter. If there is a wooly characteristic present, one should start experimenting with Mortlach. The same holds for any musty characteristic.

Casseroles!!! In essence, a casserole is a pot, usually of crockery, used not only for cooking stews but also for serving them. For that matter, Cipaille is very much a casserole. Just about anything, meat, fish or bird, can and does wind up in a casserole.

Meat loaf. This economical "dish" is excellent hot, cold or warmed over. Also, just as in the case of the stews, a meat loaf can vary considerably according to the amount and type of spices used. The consistency alone, however, will play a certain role in the selection of the proper malt Scotch and in this case one of the more traditional brands would be an excellent choice. This means a "medium" Grampian or a Lowland, and Glenturret, Tamnavulin, Glencadam, Dufftown and Glenforres come to mind.

Croquettes are basically miniature, homogeneous Cipailles. Now there are croquettes and there are croquettes. The ones in question are those where the meat or the fish is finely ground and mixed in with mashed potatoes. This mixture is then formed into patties and usually deep fried. One way or another, croquettes are much the same as pies and the taste of the potato will predominate unless the spices impart their own flavour.

Similar to croquettes, there are sausage rolls (pigs in the blanket) which are simply sausages, pork or beef, often enrobed in potatoes, rolled in bread or cracker crumbs and sometimes deep fried. They taste like croquettes, or pastry - only the consistency is different. In this case, the taste of the potato very definitely predominates. Both of these presentations require something with a little bit of character, more on the mellow side in order to give an overall taste of goodness. Balvenie or Glendronach (aged in sherry casks) is about the best. But, dollar in mind, it is a shame to use such good liquor on mundane dishes. On the other hand, it's a fine way of bringing these mundane dishes out of that category.

Mention was made of sausages and black (or blood) pudding. Before leaving this chapter something must be said for these two items. The sausage, as we know, is now not only made of pork but also beef and a number of other ingredients not the least of which are spices. Again it is suggested that, because of the variety of sausages, it is important to know them and follow the rule of thumb of cutting the heavy stuff with a malt that has enough character to do the job but is not so strong that it will add to the weight. Cragganmore or Linkwood are number one for this task. On the other hand, there is blood pudding. It is dry, mealy and has a strange taste all of its own. If nips are traditional with haggis, they are also a very good companion for blood pudding, and if that's the case, why not Cardhu?

Not much has been said about preparations such as hamburgers - if they can be called a dish! Should such an expensive beverage as malt Scotch even be considered for this kind of food? Well now, just look at some menus and see how hamburg or ground beef is disguised by sophisticated names like Swiss Steak, Salisbury Steak or Chopped Sirloin, all topped with mushrooms and onions and sauce and whatever. There is indeed an answer - trusty old Deanston.

What do we do with meat balls? Chili con carne? Hash? The only one to leave a question mark is chili con carne. With most other non-Celtic preparations it is not too difficult to come up with something legitimate as an accompanying drink. Deanston is a most trustworthy standby. But only so much can be expected. Think of curry for instance! Here's a challenge. But if you can find a complementary wine, you can be assured that there is also a malt Scotch.

As in the case of the other chapters dealing with entrées, only the better known presentations have been discussed. To have done otherwise would have entailed considerably more material without adding anything to what is intended as a guideline towards personal experimentation and discoveries in any case. However, and this is a major proviso, throughout the foregoing discourse involving meat, fish and birds, no mention has been made of what, in the minds of many, is a most important element - sauces. The Celtic kitchen will never claim to match the *cuisine continentale* for sauces. But even if it is something over which there might be little control, let this never be a reason for setting malt Scotch whisky aside. If it is a challenge for malt Scotch to claim a status equal to wine where traditional dishes are concerned, think of the challenge where haute cuisine comes into play. But that is where the finest of the fine malt Scotch whiskies can "pick up the gauntlet." *En garde*! And meet me in the next chapter...

CHAPTER 11
SAUCE AND SPICE AND EVERYTHING NICE

Sauces and spices are the two most important "additives" to any preparation and are intimately related one to the other. It was felt that dealing with them in one chapter would be more appropriate than separating them.

Sauce can have a number of meanings such as "he's into the sauce again" or "getting sauced up" or "she's a saucy little devil."Where those expressions come from matters very little, but it is not too difficult to conjure up an explanation knowing that "sauce" in the everyday usage is something that enhances or gives "zing" to a presentation that is otherwise quite ordinary. Culinary sauces are indispensable to many dishes. In some instances they disguise but, by and large, like the proper malt Scotch whisky (and yes, like a good wine) they enhance or balance a dish. Sauces come in various flavours, consistencies and colours among other things, but our prime consideration at this time is the characteristics of two types of sauces: Those that go with entrées and those that go with desserts. Their range is considerable, making it quite a challenge to select the proper malt Scotch whisky to match. It is much simpler to deal with Steak Tartar or smoked salmon where there is no sauce. But then where would the gastronomic world be without sauces for a lobster Newburg, or the Christmas turkey, Easter ham, plum pudding, and so on?

Where to start! Sauce Bearnaise? Amandine? Bourguignonne? Nicoise? Not really. That is putting the cart before the horse. It is hoped that no one's intelligence will be hurt by the suggestion that, firstly, it would be wise to understand the basic elements of sauces if only to be certain of a good match between the dish these sauces complement and the malt Scotch whiskies to be selected. Not everyone realizes the complexity and exigencies of a good sauce.

The reason for going into such detail is that to understand the sauce is to know the effect it will have on a given dish. With such knowledge, the choice of brands will be all the more judicious.

There are four elements to the base of any sauce, used singly or in combinations. These elements are fat (also oil or butter), flour, cornstarch, and a liquid (stock). From these elements usually two basic types of sauces emerge: white and brown. The basic brown sauce comes from the flour or cornstarch being "browned" or heated to a relatively high degree in a pan. The white sauce simply comes from water, clear juice, cream or milk being added to the flour as the liquid or stock. These bases come in three consistencies. Thin or runny, medium (how imaginative can you get?) and thick (what else?). These three consistencies complement their respective types of dishes whether in the balancing or enhancing mode. (Where have you heard that before!)To know the sauce is also to have a very good idea of the end result of the dish because the influence of the sauce is considerable. In making the selection of the malt Scotch, consideration must be given to the overall impact that the sauce or sauces will have on the meal as a whole.

The taste of these basic sauces is invariably planned in advance with an intended function. Unless something is added, the whites are quite bland and a good sauce chef can do wonders with them. The browns are easier to handle because they already have somewhat of a nice soft, burned or rich taste to start with. The dish to which the sauce is added will not change much other than to be a bit heavier or richer. What usually happens in such cases is that there is a tendency to take in more liquid. It is, therefore, not a sin to add a bit more water to the malt Scotch, not only to reduce the alcoholic intake but especially not to disturb the combination of food and sauce.

One of the main functions of most sauces is to moisten the dish. The drier the meat, the lighter the sauce. The blander the meat, then the more will the sauce tend to have a character of its own, thanks to the imagination of the cook. For instance, take a plank steak well beaten (it should be relatively thick to start with in order not to end up as thin as phyllo pastry) and cover it with a heavy brown sauce to which powdered mustard and white pepper have been added with a touch of red vinegar. Care to guess what brand would go well with that? How about Lagavulin diluted about twenty percent. The result is superb. But, were not the Islay malts supposed to be virtually the reserve of the crustaceans! Well, here is an exception. The trouble is that with an imaginative sauce, there may be many exceptions. Now, indeed, we can appreciate what fun can be had in matching up various brands with equally various foods.

Is there a rule of thumb? Not really, because of the virtually infinite variety of sauces once we go beyond the basics. Insofar as the basics are concerned, the principles of balancing and enhancing adhere to the general rule. Granted, that is not being very helpful, but one cannot be too careful - if only to avoid potential pitfalls as in the case of the plank steak above where the best brand traditionally belongs to another type of dish. The balancing or enhancing decision will be left up to your imagination once we get beyond what follows.

Light, medium and heavy meats were discussed earlier but nothing was mentioned about attendant sauces. A quick check at this time will not do any harm. Light meats can include beef, fish or fowl with veal probably the lightest of them all. Smelt and haddock can well speak for all white, non-oily fish as can chicken stand in for all fowl. Steaks and roasts cover the medium meats. Mullet, trout and perch are mediums for fish and the brown meats of domestic fowl fit in here very well. The heavies are easily recognized: steak tartar and other exotic preparations, smoked salmon, kipper, herring and wild birds.

With light meats and a light sauce, a middle-weight brand such as Knockando or a young Glenfarclas is an excellent choice. As the sauce gets heavier, ease off with a Littlemill or a Deanston. Where you have medium meats with light sauce, remember that the meats will start to come through. If the sauce is just a moistener, it is best buried with a good brand whether your choice is to balance or enhance. If the sauce is a true complement to the dish, then there is a challenge indeed. In fact, something with a bit more character than usual might be in order. For example, Cardhu will do but something like Clynelish or Dalmore might be better. This will establish a good rapport between the food and the drink. When a heavy sauce is matched up with a medium meat then there is the choice of increasing the strength of the drink, going to a heavier brand or simply taking the easy way out and going light with a weak Rosebank. One of the favourites for a good gastronomical fit is a Linkwood or a Cragganmore. The heavy meats become a challenge. The taste really comes through and it would take a powerful or highly flavoured sauce to hide the taste of wild birds for instance. That is why most sauces here will be light. In many cases, no sauce is used and meats are prepared in a manner that will take advantage of natural juices. If a heavy sauce is encountered, the usual appropriate selection would be a very light young uisgage but with the strength to maintain character. Tullibardine and Bunnahabhain would be two good selections.

Though desserts have their own chapter it is felt that any sauce related thereto should be discussed here. Of any dish, on any table, at any time, desserts and their sauces are overall enhancers. In this respect, the dessert sauce is very special in that it not only must enhance or balance its own dish, but it must not interfere with the entrée. Desserts by their very nature are sweet. The sauces more often than not are going to be the same. To borrow a page from the oenologists, dessert wines are invariably sweet.Portos are often considered sweet dessert wines. Malaga or Sperone portos are considered among the sweetest and nothing in the malt world is nearly as sweet as any of those. But Glendronach and Macallan beyond the eighteen-year-old mark are incredibly smooth.

By way of summary, and it bears repeating, you must imagine the taste of the dish and sauce combination and then determine whether that combination can be enhanced or balanced. It is folly to try and overpower unless it is a foregone conclusion that the cook is a dead loss where the craft is concerned. The main dish sauces might range from those mentioned earlier to a bechamel, pineapple, poulette, butter, caper, hollandaise, giblet, gravy, bread sauce, cucumber dressing, mushroom, onion, sauce piquante, curry, olive, spanish, chateaubriand, tomato, ravigotte and glazings for meats. Any good cook book will give you the details for these sauces and open the door to many more. This is just a sample of what lies ahead for you. In this respect, do remember what was said about sweet sauces for desserts and take care for a proper match.

Inasmuch as the cook has recourse to myriad sauces, there are almost as many spices with which to enhance the entrée. Our challenge then is all the greater because, in diluting any of the various brands of malt whiskies we end up with as many "liquors" as there are sauces and spices.

There are two categories of spices. Herbs and seeds. The herbs are generally quite well known and the ones most used are bay leaf, dill, fennel, marjoram, mint, parsley, saffron, sage, savory, sweet basil, tarragon and thyme. Don't forget that we are dealing with sauces here and not stuffings. Already we have eliminated sage, savory and thyme. Bay leaves are subtle. Dill and fennel are not but they don't wind up in sauces all too often.Marjoram is musty sweet, not unlike Mortlach. Mint, of course, is the traditional spice for lamb and may be used for any number of other sauces in conjunction with other herbs and seeds. Be careful of this one. Mint is distinct, unique and should not be overpowred, principally because the dish it accompanies requires this very flavour.

The idea is to enhance the whole exercise with a subtle, delicate, yet not sweet malt Scotch whisky. A well-aged Auchentoshan or Glengoyne reduced by as much as forty percent would be excellent. The only question is whether or not to dilute a sixty dollar malt!

Parsley is also subtle, though less than bay leaves. It is not only neutral but a good herb to neutralize other spices such as garlic. Its own taste or effect is not unlike that of marjoram. Saffron is mainly a colouring. Curry is another spice that is sweet and musty.

All the herbs so far would respond well to Auchentoshan and Glengoyne and some others of the same region and strength. But there is one herb left that is very different. This one leaves a hot and pungent taste and has considerable effect on any dish. Tarragon. It is a worthy match for the Islay malts and while we are not necessarily looking at Ardbeg or Laphroig, any of the others reduced about twenty-five percent should do the trick.

Where seeds are concerned, cardamom and nutmeg are really not main course spices and fit much better in the flavour and extracts categories, most suitable for desserts. The most common seeds used to flavour sauces are cloves, curry, mace, mustard, paprika and pepper. Only cloves and curry might create problems because of their strength. Pepper, we know, can be hot but there is little flavour. Much the same can be said for mace and paprika. But think of cloves in ham along with the mustard and brown sugar and you virtually eliminate all malts with the exception of Balvenie as is or a slightly diluted Macallan or Glendronach (sherry cask). Curry is a true challenge, and of the two brands that come to mind, Ladyburn and Glenburn, only the former is still available. At this writing it is difficult to come up with even a specific "vatting"other than to suggest two thirds Balvenie with one third Tobermory and add about five percent water.

Some eyebrows are raised?What is all this about mixing malt Scotchs?Mortal sin - capital error - an original no-no. In reality this is very much the principle of "doing your own thing" as set out in Chapter 5 (at the risk of being labelled a heretic), but do start off your experiments with malts as they are. No liquor is sacrosanct and where your taste suggests something a bit different, go ahead and experiment. On the other hand, bear in mind that "vatting" is a very, very delicate business requiring many long years of experience. But then, one must start somewhere...

Like curry, the vegetable flavourings are different than seeds and herbs. Here we have much more potent material going into the sauces. Onions and garlic are the heavyweights and what was said about not trying to overpower any "additive" which has considerable character of its own still holds. Ride with the tide; it's more fun. Garlic is a dandy, and though the Bretons are well known in the Celtic realms for their onions, garlic is better known by those of the Latin bloodlines. Nevertheless, let us pick up the gauntlet and go out on a limb, suggesting a Bunnahabhain or Bruichladdich. Again bear in mind that garlic has a character very much its own and one should not try to overpower it. Indeed, there is no certainty that it can be done! All that can be said is that garlic is not common to the land of the malt Scotch. But if any attempt is to be made to prove this drink worthy of being on the dinner table, then everything has to be tried - doesn't it?

Celery is a vegetable flavouring which is nice and smooth. There is no question of overpowering here and the natural flavour of the entrée will determine the brand to be selected. Tomatoes will find their way into a sauce quite easily (as in a spaghetti sauce, with ravioli, or rigatoni for example). These dishes are not common to the Celtic world, but tomato sauce and meat loaf is a natural combination. Fortunately, tomatoes are not overpowering and any medium malt will go well. Milton-Duff or Dufftown...that's the idea.

One would think that lemon and orange are definitely dessert sauce material and they are. But their versatility makes them naturals for some fowl, as in canard à l'orange, and in some sauces for fish dishes. Because of the citric nature of these juices, something bordering the Islay character would be recommended. Why not some of the southern Caledonians (see the list in the chapter on origins). In plain language, Cardhu, Oban and Bladnoch commend themselves to your palate.

CHAPTER 12
DESSERT ME NOT

Suet pudding and Macallan. Sheer unadulterated heaven on earth. But what about the rest of the meal? It is amazing the extent to which the dessert may affect the entrée. Listen carefully to the comments of guests or patrons next time you are out for a meal or when you yourself are hosting. Generally, the comments will be about the meal as a whole, but quite often the dessert will be singled out. Not that the entrée was inferior, but the dessert is what the guests often remember most.

There is no doubt that dessert does have considerable bearing on a meal. As suggested previously, the meal as a whole is a combination of many factors. The main course or entrée will, naturally, be the principal factor, but the dessert or cheese, or both, will also have a noticeable effect on the overall character of the repast. Having added up all the factors beforehand, the selection of one brand to cover all the elements of the meal should be that much easier.

As a good hostess or host, you will have taken care to balance the main course with the proper dessert, in which case the selection of malt Scotch for dessert, if there is to be a a different brand to that of the entrée, should not be difficult. Generally, stay with the brand used for the main course, thereby avoiding the danger of offsetting the effect of the final element of the meal on the whole.

It is strange that we talk of desserts as a condition sine qua non to any meal when in fact quite often the ordinary day to day meal goes without dessert, or if there is one, it is not specifically matched to the main course. It is reasonable to assume therefore that where a specific dessert has been prepared, the meal has been a special one and great care has been exercised to ensure balance. It is also reasonable to assume then that the malt Scotch experience would take place only on such occasions, much like the *raison d'être* for the selection of *grands vins*. It must be remembered, however, that there are also *vins de table* or *ordinaires*, which are part of the common meal in many countries. One can do the same with malt Scotch.

Kindly recall two things mentioned earlier in this work. The first is that malt Scotch whisky at one time was the common table drink, and the second is that the revival of that practice should be given serious consideration. Therefore, dessert or no dessert - bring on the uisge.

What is so special about desserts, you ask? Having swallowed the last mouthful of a black forest, or a bagatelle, or a trifle (may the good Lord always bless the booze leftovers), do we not look across the table and with mock repentance say, "Oooh, I shouldn't have had that dessert but it was simply sooo delicious, wasn't it?" And everybody nods in assent. The fact is that the dessert was indeed delicious and was a complement to the meal, as it was meant to be. A point to keep in mind then is that it is dangerous to upset any balance that has been established. That is one of the reasons, probably the main reason, why dessert wines, like the desserts themselves, are usually quite sweet. That should give us yet another challenge because the sweet and mellow malts are few and far between. Some would say that, on the contrary, the matter has been simplified because there are no malts which are that sweet. Maybe so, but the problem is solved by observing the basic principle of staying with the brand served with the entrée. Here's why...

For the most part, desserts are sweet and filling. Those that have sauces may be even more so as in the case of plum pudding. Though there is usually a common trait of smoothness, mellowness, or sweetness, desserts do vary and it is intriguing that this variety comes not from the dish itself but from the flavour and consistency. This phenomenon may best be explained by the fact that a lemon pie is not sour. It is tart and sweet but still tastes lemony.

If you are at a loss, then stick to the brand used for the entrée. This very basic rule has been stated three times already; sorry for the repetition, but it is so basic it does bear repeating. If you are going to follow this advice then consider diluting it a little bit more. Keep in mind that the object of the dessert is to leave the table with a taste of well-balanced sweetness. And the reason for that is that a sweet taste seldom invites more food or excites the appetite, unless the tooth is very sweet indeed.

Generally, desserts other than whole fruit desserts come with a crust of some kind or a crumb pastry which may or may not be sufficiently moistened by the filling or sauce. In any case, the crumb and the crust will invariably be recognized and maybe require a bit of additional moistening This is where watered-down malt comes in, just like the dessert wine. Remember, if the malt Scotch is to be watered down, this means selecting a brand that can stand it without losing everything.

In the case of puddings, moisture not only depends on the dish itself but also on the generosity of the host or hostess with the sauce. Puddings that are inherently dry are rare indeed if they do not require additional moisture. These can stand a slightly stronger drink because they will either have a strong character of their own or have virtually no taste at all with all the delight being in the consistency (as with our old friend suet pudding). On the other hand, a stronger spice pudding suggests a return to a weaker drink.

Cakes are virtually all dry. Cake as a dessert in itself is not that common and most of those that are served as a dessert will have a very distinct flavour. This also suggests a weaker drink, one that will not obliterate the flavour of the cake.

Pies come in as many varieties as there are stars in the sky. The great majority of pies will be moist so it is better to steer clear of anything that might detract from the taste, unless it is something quite indigestible in which case it should be washed down with a good belt of pure Ardbeg. The cook might not appreciate the implication but the smile on your face will go a long way in repairing the damage.

Pies will be sweet, tart, or neutral. With the sweets there is little choice but to go for a heavier brand aged in sherry casks such as Glendronach or Macallan, reduced by as much as twenty-five percent. The tarts respond well to a light Lowland also diluted, and once again Deanston will acquit itself admirably. The neutral tastes will be well accomodated by a stronger Lowland less diluted, such as a Glengoyne or Littlemill.

Puddings are greatly influenced by the sauce. If there is no sauce and the pudding is dry, then a little bit of experimenting can be done. Tobermory, Bunnahabhain and Bruichladdich are good candidates for an "oily" type of pudding such as coconut or date.

The "mealy" kind of pudding responds well to a slightly diluted Oban or Cardhu. Where there is a sauce, then do the best you can with what there is. Go by the general rule.

Little has been said about fruits and custards. Fruits will have their own flavours or will be considerably spiced. Don't touch the malts. Virtually the same can be said for custards.

In summary, the dessert being what it is - something with considerable character of its own, mainly sweetness - there is not much that can be recommended other than to go with the malt Scotch selected for the main course. Where there is room for choice, be on the cautious side and remain with a sweet Grampian or a heavy Lowland. Be patient - the pousse-café can be out of this world. There is little doubt in my mind that you will agree.

CHAPTER 13
FOR AULD LANG SYNE

When a function draws to a close, in many instances our thoughts are drawn to the words of the immortal Scottish bard, Robbie Burns..."We'll tak' a cup o' kindness yet..." These words are particularly appropriate at the end of a meal, any meal, that has been enhanced with malt Scotch whisky. The sheer company of malt Scotch paves a highway to heaven through the mists of...

Glenlivet, Glendronach and Oban,
    Not to mention the beauteous Macallan.

As a *pousse-café*, malt Scotch is in a class by itself. It is said that the epitome of gastronomy is to leave the table satisfied yet not bloated and with a rich clean taste in the mouth. There is nothing wrong with fine liqueurs; however, for many, the high sugar and alcohol content may well be the cause of one glorious, snapping headache the next morning, (keeping in mind that the dinner wine alone, if there was wine at the dinner table, can do the trick). Personally, my preference was a good sweet porto, particularly Malaga or Sperone - till I met up with the likes of Glendronach (sherry cask) or Macallan. The taste of the wines was sweet and rich compared to the smooth, clean palate of malt Scotch and the cleanest may well be Balvenie. Many will take me to task for ignoring, so it seems, the Scottish fine liqueurs such as Drambuie and Glayva. But do not be hasty...read on.

The governing principles for malt Scotch as a *pousse-café* are a combination of what has been stated for the apéritif and the meal itself. Usually the weather and the season are a great influence as to what will taste best, if only from a psychological point of view. For example, if it is a cold and rainy November evening, Balvenie or Glengoyne may not be the best brands to sip by the fireplace even after a heavy meal. A nice Milton-Duff or a heavier, yet clean, Glendronach (original) would do a better job of warming the cockles of your heart. It would not be out of place to think of a Lagavulin, but that is one brand for which a taste has to be acquired. When it has, then there is none other. Also, one can settle for a Bowmore or a slightly smoother Tobermory. And all this without taking the meal into consideration.

Now, about the influence of the meal. There is no doubt that it does have a bearing. As suggested previously the meal as a whole is a combination of many factors. The main course will, assuredly, be the principal factor, but the dessert or cheese, or a combination thereof, will also have a noticeable effect on the overall character of the meal. All of the factors have to be added up and the sum of the characteristics should be the governing indicator for your selection.

In most instances the main course will have been balanced with the proper dessert. There may be cheese to follow but at this time there is usually only the dessert with which to contend. If the dessert does balance well with the main course, then the choice is not difficult. Stay with the brand of the main course unless the pousse-café follows at least half an hour later. Then it is a question of mood and atmosphere. If the meal was light then it is usually a good thing to stay with a lighter brand. In every case, however, this is where you are looking for a brand with a lot of staying power, be it Lowland or Highland. Never mind about the Islay. They have so much staying power you are reminded of their presence even the next day. The heavier meals strangely enough are very nicely complemented by an equally heavy brand. In such cases it is wise to follow the rule of extending the main course brand with an Islay. The Ardbeg tops the list but Bunnahabhain or Tobermory would have a better tapering-off effect with the desired lingering after-taste. Usually one cannot go wrong with the heavier Grampians or north Caledonians (my grouping) such as Clynelish or particularly Dalmore.

If some cheese has been added to close off the meal, there are the makings of an interesting situation. The gourmet will, of course, be very pleased, particularly with a medium or soft cheese. It has been said that the purpose of cheese following a meal is to help digestion by having the bacteria participate in the breaking down process. It is felt, however, that if the meal has been heavy yet tasty, cheese will tend to draw away from it and certainly not leave that rich, clean taste. If, on the other hand, the meal has been light and seems somewhat incomplete in spite of the dessert, then cheese may be very welcome. Cheese does not really add to a meal unless it is in keeping with the overall flavour. Matching a cheese to the main course is not an easy task because cheese, no matter what kind, has a character strong enough to stand on its own, as mentioned in Chapter 6, (unless you have one of the "plastic" variety).

Then there is the matter of the expense and the timing. A gourmet hostess will offer an appropriate cheese but there is an ever-present danger that the selection will be made on the basis of brand reputation rather than the worth of the cheese itself. How often do you see a Camembert after a meal? Almost always. Yet it does not go too well with any shellfish, or salmon, or cod, or smelt, and so on. That is just one example. In the final analysis, the cheese can easily become a mini meal in itself. Be very careful of balancing between the cheese and the dessert/main course combination.

Whether there is a balance or not, remember that cheese, because of the work it does in the digestive process, will more than likely erase any of the meal's aftertaste. For this reason, go back to the "Cheese Please" chapter and review the selection suggestions so that the aftertaste of the cheese will also be erased. Thus you will be left with the most pleasant taste of all - that of the malt Scotch.

The mark of the real connoisseur is to select a cheese which will be in "conjunction" and once again the choice of the pousse-café will not be too difficult. However, if they are in "opposition," then it will be all the more important to follow the advice in the paragraph above.

It is doubtful that there will be much of a selection of malt Scotch at the best of times unless you happen to be a member of a club or society of collectors. My suggestion in such cases is to make sure that the brand selected for the dinner table is sufficiently cut so that it will not only blend in with the meal, but so that it can also be enjoyed full strength, as an after-dinner drink. This increases the aftertaste and maintains the "lineage" of the meal drink.

Malt Scotch is unique in the world in this respect. There are very few wines, if any, that could be cut for the purpose of accompanying a main course, and do a good job of it, and then be taken full strength as a pousse-café. In fact, with the variety of wines available and the assigned role to each, it would take an oenological heretic to do what has been suggested here.

It would, likewise, be very foolish to suggest that fine liqueurs do not have their place in the world of food and drink. Not only are they excellent in their role of *pousse-café* because of the extremely wide range of flavours that can enhance a meal, but they are also perfect as cocktail ingredients. However, because of their very nature, they frequently produce hangovers. The main reason is that they are either a mixture of an essence concentrate with grain alcohol, or they are a distillate of a fruit, flower or seed mash. The limited amount of dehydrogenase and other enzymes in the body oftentimes cannot cope, and the fusel oil congener will have free reign as a headache producer.

Speaking of liqueurs, the promise made to you earlier is now being honoured. Probably the best known liqueur coming from the Highlands is Drambuie. It reputedly follows the personal recipe that Bonnie Prince Charlie gave to the clan MacKinnon as a recompense for their services in his time of need. But there are other liqueurs such as Glayva, Glenturret Liqueur, Heather Cream, Lochanora and Oran Mhor. The taste of these drinks is wonderful, but they are heavy and sweet. For those that can take them - go ahead. One thing to remember is that they are something unto themselves and after coffee, well... they do go down nicely. But like many other fine liqueurs, they can be the cause of the most horrendous migraines imaginable. And that is why many have come to stay with the malt Scotch from the beginning to the end. It bears repeating that *uisge beatha* is truly a complete, pure and salubrious liquor.

Many will contend, with reason, that the range of flavours in fine liqueurs is wider than it is for malt Scotch whiskies. It is further contended that on that basis, malt Scotch should not be considered as an after-dinner drink. What then do we do with Cognac, one of the more traditional after-dinner drinks to which malt Scotch whisky is often compared? Though malt Scotch whisky does not have the range of flavours found in liqueurs, it is much wider than that found in Cognac! All challenges welcome. Many claim that the range in Cognacs is oh, so subtle. The connoisseur will find that it is oh, more so with malt Scotch. It is there - but it must be discovered. When found, it gives a sense of "knowing" - yet another experience, another page in the book of knowledge.

Surely this is also reason enough to stop comparing malt Scotch to Cognac and start comparing Cognac to malt Scotch!

Finally, there are a number of brands that stand out as after-dinner drinks as such - principally the dark, rich Grampians, and for some the sharp smoke of the Islands. If all the rules have been followed, and in time they will - by rote - the sheer delight of the cleansing fumes will envelop your being like the gentle mist stealing over the moor, or the moonlit sea washing the craigs to the skirl of the pipes faintly wafting over the glen.

NOTES ON PART II

Part II is in essence a series of appendices to Part I. Chapter 14 is a complement to Chapter 2, setting out how to conduct nosings and tastings. The brands that are recommended as samples are readily available at the present time but there can be no guarantee that it will always be so. Nosing and tasting forms appear as Annex B.

Chapter 15 gives a few suggestions as to why and how a malt Scotch whisky society might be formed. It is the story of **An Quaich**, the society that I started in 1983, and records its successes and difficulties.

Chapter 16, together with its tables, is a resume of my own survey of malts and their interaction with food. Where there are blanks or no comments, it does not mean that a particular malt does not go well with a given food. So far as I am concerned, they are all more than acceptable. I am merely passing on what I have found to be the best.

I have deliberately refrained from summarizing the characteristics of the malts themselves because the reader will find this in any other book dealing with malt Scotch whisky. Why do I NOT include it anyway? I think that it would be nice for the reader to get the opinion of somebody else and I would be repeating what so many others have done. In any case, Chapter 15 is in itself somewhat of a summary.

Some brands are missing? Of course they are. My research facilities are limited and obtaining the rarer brands has been and continues to be quite difficult. Nevertheless, it is a worthwhile effort and the aficionado will be amply rewarded.

The last annex consists of a number of maps essential to the identification of the malt Scotch-producing areas. If "a picture is worth a thousand words," readers will find this material very helpful in remembering and differentiating one area from the other.

B.E.P.

CHAPTER 14
HOW TO ORGANIZE
NOSINGS AND TASTINGS

Chapter 2 went a long way in providing information on how to taste and nose malt Scotch whisky. But that is not the whole story. The pleasures that malt Scotch whisky can offer are enhanced if experienced in a group and this chapter will show you how. It is assumed that being a guide, this chapter will be copied from time to time. On this assumption a number of comments made in earlier parts of this book will be repeated here.

All too often tastings are done to determine if a brand is better than another. Although this is a familiar procedure with other types of alcoholic beverages, it does not hold in the case of malt Scotch whisky because, in essence, there is no such thing as a bad one.

It is not a good idea to compare one malt Scotch whisky with another or one year or batch with another of the same brand. By definition they do not vary.Indeed, one of the objects in the distillation process is to maintain the *same* high quality, taste, colour, body, legs and so on, year after year after year. And this has been achieved for over two centuries.

For one person to say that Ardbeg is better than Macallan or that Glenforres is better than Poit Dhubh is not acceptable because another person with equal knowledge of the matter might say just the opposite and both in *their own opinion* would be correct. The judgement is subjective and based on the fact that the first person prefers smoke and peat to something full-bodied, balanced and mellow. The second person prefers the opposite - who is right? Is one malt Scotch better than the other? No. And the reason is now obvious.

However, let us suppose that a competition were to be set up with such parameters as: excellence as an after-dinner drink; the drink must be a distillate of a fruit or a cereal; and the drink must not be a blend of another spirit. Then, even these three brief parameters would allow a proper comparison between, say, a Grand Napoleon cognac and a Balvenie 18-year-old malt Scotch whisky. On this basis, the "games" of nosing and tasting are quite interesting.

A typical nosing 'station'.

AIM OF NOSINGS AND TASTINGS

On the basis of the above, and for our purposes, the terms "nosing" and "tasting" should be defined more precisely. A "nosing" is the procedure whereby the characteristics of a liquid are identified and categorized by the sense of sight and smell only.Considerable information has already been given on the technique of nosing and will, therefore, be reviewed only very briefly later on. In "tasting" we also seek to identify and categorize the characteristics of a liquid, but this time by the sense of taste. It should be repeated that in the case of malt Scotch whisky, (unlike many other spirits), one does NOT spit out the sample.

It is important to note that though the nosing process is an integral part of a tasting, the opposite is not true in that there is no tasting as part of a nosing. Also there is the fundamental difference that a tasting should not involve more than three samples - four at the most. In the case of a nosing, a comfortable number is six.

The aim of nosing and tasting malt Scotch whiskies is very much the same as for wines. An individual wishes to get to recognize the inherent qualities of the spirit in order to draw the most satisfaction from its ingestion.

Through repeated trial and error it becomes possible to recognize a wide variety of characteristics that readily identify one brand of malt Scotch whisky from another. This can be accomplished in a relatively short time with a great degree of satisfaction. The judicious Master of the Quaich will therefore select brands that will accomplish this and lead his followers through a series of such functions to the point where there will be no difficulty in recognizing an appreciable number of brands from the same region - much to the delight of all.

As opposed to wines, malt Scotch is, in the minds of many, a new kid on the street, particularly where the accompaniment to food is concerned. Yet another aim of nosings and tastings is to match up, through the process of recalling the taste of various dishes, a particular brand of malt Scotch whisky with a specific dish - and then try it!

THE PROCESS

The Master of the Quaich must prepare well. Contrary to general belief and practice, a nosing is more complicated and requires considerably more expertise than a tasting. The reasons are obvious. In a nosing, an individual has only the senses of sight and smell to go by. Factors to be considered include colour, legs (tears), attack (on the nose), presence and persistence. Although this represents a considerable amount of information, it is less than half the story. Although there remains only one more sense, that of taste, it is the vital one in that it confirms what the eyes and nose have first perceived and reveals four other characteristics i.e., body, bite, balance and aftertaste, (the balance being the combination of smoke and peat).

Tasting: The Master should therefore consider a tasting first. After two or three tastings the characteristics will become very evident and readily identified. Tasters should be provided with an evaluation sheet such as was referred to previously (found at Annex A).

Tasters should record not only their impressions but also the comments of the Master and retain the sheets as permanent records for reference purposes. It won't take long before these records become history and samples identified from memory. Here is the way it's done.

It is advisable to select three brands that can be readily identified. Of course, the brands should be such as to be readily available at any time. In the world of malt Scotch whisky, this may be a lot more easily said than done. Certain brands may be recommended here, but there is no guarantee that they will be available in every outlet in the country. In such instances, it is a question of making the best out of a difficult situation. Every effort has been made here to suggest what is possible.

Probably the most easily identifiable brands are the malt Scotch whiskies coming from the Islands. In order of distinctiveness ranging from the most iodoform, peaty and smoky to the least there is Ardbeg, Lagavulin, Laphroig, Talisker, Oban, Bunnahabhain, Bruichladdich, Tobermory, Isle of Jura and Highland Park. Ardbeg is difficult to obtain and at this writing the most likely candidates would be any one of Lagavulin, Laphroig or Talisker.

Next would be a selection from the Highlands. Care should be exercised not to go to any of the more "special" brands of Highland malts such as Macallan, Balvanie or Glendronach aged in sherry casks. A traditionally strong Grampian such as THE Glenlivet, or Glenfiddich, would be a natural. There is a plethora of others but not as readily available. The third category is the Lowland malt and the one that is probably most representative and available would be Glenkinchie or Rosebank.

Each category will have its colour. Emphasizing some of the details found in Chapter 2, it will be noted that the Island and the Highland malts may have similar colouring, but the legs and the aroma will quickly separate them. The light colour of the Lowland malts is a "dead give-away."The ritual explained in the chapter mentioned above should now be followed. Each characteristic should be noted on the evaluation sheet as suggested thereon, rating them from one to five in order of "presence."

Having selected the brands, the Master may wish to identify the brands beforehand and lead the tasters through the various characteristics of each label pointing out the differences. On the other hand, the Master might prefer to reveal the names of the brands only after. One way or the other, there should be a quick review of the main characteristics of each category so that the tasters can at least have an idea of what they are looking for. The latter method makes for a slightly more interesting session without defeating the instructional aspect.

Each taster should have three glasses. The glasses should be numbered 1, 2 and 3. The Master should know which sample is in which glass but this should not be known to the tasters. This is where the Master can make a game or a competition of the function and keep scores. As the tasters get better, not only will they be able to identify samples readily but opinions and discussion should be invited as to the type of food that could accompany the samples and the amount of dilution suggested.

Once proficiency with the "basic three" types of brands has been established, the Master should then get into the more subtle tastes still found within those categories. For example, an Oban is not so easily distinguishable from Clynelish or Dalmore or Cardhu, and a Glengoyne is a rather strong Lowland malt. Even some experts could be thrown by this combination. This could be considered as step two, and the number of combinations is considerable though controllable. Step three involves the expertise category but it also has levels. The step consists of staying with a category and trying to identify the differences between Lagavulin, Laphroig and Talisker. Once this had been achieved then go for differences between an easily recognizable brand (still within the Island category) and two more subtle ones. The Islands and the Lowlands will not give much scope, but watch out with the Highland malts. Here the areas of Speyside, Tayside, and northern Highland or Campbeltown will not provide appreciable clues. The Master will have his or her hands full principally with colour, body and mostly aftertaste, largely because of two "masking" factors - sherry cask aging and vatting.

A final word on tasting. Many tasters of other spirits do not swallow the sample. They rinse the mouth and follow a ritual of eating bread all to neutralize the taste that is left. Well, that may all be good and a rinse with a bit of bread may help neutralize the taste, but with malt Scotch whisky it is going to take some neutralizing. However, spitting out the sample will not help at all, particularly when so much depends on the aftertaste which can only be properly acquired if the sample is swallowed and reaches the warmth of the stomach. Therefore, do swallow and enjoy.

Nosing: If that much fun can be provided with only three samples at a tasting, think of what can be accomplished with six samples at a nosing. However, it may not be as much fun because there is no tasting. A challenge? Definitely. And again, it is a question of the Master leading the nosers gently down the path.

The set-up is important of course and the traditional one is to have six samples well identified and in a row each behind a glass. So long as the brands are numbered (from 1 to 6), the glasses need not be, though there is merit in doing so. The front row of six glasses should contain the same samples as the back row of glasses but not in the same order. These glasses should be lettered from A to F. A typical nosing card is shown in Annex B.

Unlike a tasting where the tasters are sitting and time is of no consequence, nosings take place standing in most cases and not everybody has a nosing station. The average time for nosing one sample is two minutes so that an overall average of fifteen minutes might be allotted for nosing six samples. Normally, a nosing station cannot accommodate much more than four nosers at the same time. The ideal is two. This means that there will be some slack time for a number of nosers and this is where the Master should

The author (centre) with two founding members of An Quaich, F. Millotte (left) and P. Kumar (right). (Citizen photo: Bruno Schlumberger)

be providing some hints or bringing to mind some characteristics to be looking for.

For a first try, the samples, again on the premise of availability, should be fairly distinctive particularly as to colour, surface tension and aroma. Here we need a very strong Island malt such as Ardbeg, Lagavulin or Talisker. The Lowland should also be distinctive, particularly as to colour. Glenkinchie again comes to the fore. There should be one Highland aged in Sherry casks if only for colour. These are rich amber. Macallan and Glendronach come to mind. Next would be very light-coloured Grampians such as Mortlach, Springbank or Tamnavulin. Taste alone will require a stronger type of Highland malt such as Inchgower, Glendronach (original) and Lochnagar to be compared with a Clynelish or Dalmore. This is the easy range. Unfortunately they are not always all available and some compromise will have to be made. In such instances the Master should use discretion as to how much information and hints can be given the nosers without spoiling the exercise.

While all this is going on, sight should never be lost of the wonderful experiences that await the nosers and tasters when the appropriate food can be matched up to the liquor and vice versa. On that line of thought and in keeping with the frugal nature of the Scots, there comes to mind a question that is often asked of me. What do you do with the nosing samples? My answer is that I make up a "quencher."Since it is not appropriate to put the samples back into each bottle, I pour them all into a pitcher, add half as much water, and serve. If nothing else, it is interesting - and I have yet to experience an aficionado refusing a free drink!

Now that you have been initiated to the wonders of malt Scotch whisky, you may ask why they have remained a secret for so long. There are numerous reasons. One of the first comments that we made was that, in its own home, malt Scotch was ignored until relatively recently. Its availability is unreliable and its sales represent only a very small volume of agents' revenues. But the situation is changing for the better. Societies such as **An Quaich** are trying to remedy the matter and this is dealt with in the next chapter. So, read on and find out how you can join the trend and have Whisky with Dinner.

A typical Scottish distillery.

CHAPTER 15
AN QUAICH

The reason for writing this chapter is because of the number of requests I have received from interested individuals: how to go about getting a particular brand of malt Scotch whisky, how to get to know about malt Scotch, and so on. I smile and say that **AN QUAICH** would no doubt be able to provide just about all the answers. This, of course, leads to further questions as to what **AN QUAICH** is and what it does.

Seven years ago at this writing I went to a local Rare Wines and Spirits outlet of the Liquor Board to get myself a bottle of Glendronach only to be told that it was no longer available. I asked if it would be long before I could get it again but there just didn't seem to be an answer. I then asked if there was any way that I could get a bottle, even if it meant getting it directly from Scotland. The answer was "yes" but that I would have to go through the Private Stock Order Department of the Liquor Board.

A telephone call to the Ontario Liquor Board headquarters in Toronto confirmed the procedure. However, I was not prepared for the requirement of buying a whole case! It was probably a bit naïve on my part to think that I would be able to get just a few bottles on an export basis from Scotland. So I went ahead with the case, reconciled to the fact that I would at least have a good supply. Or so I thought.

One day shortly thereafter, I was discussing spirits with some friends and happened to mention my acquisition. Much to my surprise, two of them asked me if I would mind selling a few bottles from my case. Realizing that this would reduce the cost considerably and still leave me with a substantial reserve, I readily agreed. A few days later, another friend asked if he could also have a bottle, and again I agreed. By the end of the week, of the twelve bottles making up the case, I had only one left!

A pewter 'quaich' — ancient Scottish drinking vessel.

It was then that I recalled an excellent article on malt Scotch whisky by Sinclair McKay in the gourmet magazine *A la Carte*. Among other things he made the suggestion that brands not otherwise available in the Rare Wines and Spirits outlets might be acquired at reasonable cost by getting people together and importing as a society. Reference was made to the Opimian Society.

This prompted further telephone calls to a few more friends and within a matter of hours I had enough interest for another case. The Liquor Board was contacted immediately and a second case was added to my original order. I was lucky. When the order arrived some three months later it was suggested that we should have a get-together to split the "booty."

In preparing for this event it was further suggested that we might form a club and order various brands more often. In fact one of the original participants had tried to get some Talisker only to be told that it was out of stock. Could we order some? Now that was a dicey question because Talisker is a little different from most of the other malt Scotch whiskys. But, sure enough, there was a sufficient number of takers to put in an order for a case. This in turn gave rise to the merits of having "tastings" of other brands in order to get to know more about them.

The idea was appealing. Though I had been sipping this kind of Scotch whisky for over thirty years, acquiring a fair knowledge of some seventy brands, here was an opportunity to get acquainted with so many more brands yet unknown to me. And all this within a circle of common interest. Very obviously samples were needed. The equally obvious source of information was the Scotch Whisky Association. Correspondence with London was enchanting and a contact was established with the SWA (Scotch Whisky Association) in Canada. A few samples of Linkwood and Cragganmore were provided free of charge. Here indeed was somebody interested in promoting their product, and by golly, we would surely help. Both these brands had been absent from Canada for a good while. They were both well known to me and I knew that they would be well received at the tasting that had been planned. They went over very well and a sizeable order was placed with the Private Stock Department of the Liquor Control Board of Ontario. That order also took three months - but that was sheer luck as I would learn later. The whole exercise had been unplanned good fortune. Further samples were impossible to get - the reasons given were many and varied.

By now our group had grown to approximately thirty members and had become duly recognized as a tasting society by the Liquor Board. We had a constitution (see Annex C) and we were meeting on a regular basis, some members ordering their favourites, others quite willing to experiment.

We settled in to what we thought would be a nice quiet routine: meet four times a year, have a tasting of some new brands brought in by Vintages (the specialty outlet of the liquor board) or through our own Tasting Committee, enjoy a good meal, camaraderie, and so on. That lasted six months.

Our first inkling of problems surfaced in May of 1987 and it did not come from the lack of samples. At that May meeting, another sizeable order (sizeable for us - thirty-six bottles) was placed through the LCBO with a reasonable assurance that we could expect the order to arrive in September. After all, four and a half months is a respectable wait. However, only half the order arrived. Answers were difficult to come by as to when the remainder of my order could be expected. Needless to say, there were a number of exchanges with the LCBO and for the first time I was told that three-month deliveries were just plain luck and that there could be no guarantee for anything less than six months. I must say that the people I dealt with bent over backwards to be helpful. My own conclusion at this time is that the whole system leaves much to be desired and is most frustrating unless one knows the "ins" and "outs," the "whys" and "wherefores." It has taken me four years of intense research, correspondence and visits to Scotland, to understand anything about the marketing and economics of the industry. Many of the problems are legitimate but there is also the priority of profits.

Orders were submitted to the LCBO with replies from Scotland taking ages, some indicating that a brand was no longer available (to the Canadian market), or that only minimum orders of ten, twenty or fifty cases would be considered, and so on. Surely, we thought, there must be a misunderstanding somewhere. Surveys were showing that Scotch whisky markets were down; our own inquiries showed an untapped market. We decided to write to the distilleries directly.

An Quaich wrote to the Scotch Whisky Association in England to get a list of distillery addresses. SWA was as helpful as they could be but the list we received contained the addresses of members only. We were referred to the SWA representatives in Canada; but these were the same people who represented a specific distributor, the Distillers' Company (Canada) Limited (now the United Distillers' Group). Was it reasonable to expect them to promote the product of competitors? In spite of the potential conflict I must say that cooperation has been excellent - though understandably not unlimited. Searching for agents in Canada was another exercise that produced very limited results. Provincial associations either did not reply or did not know. We were quite taken aback that some distilleries in Canada who are official agents for Scottish distilleries openly admitted that they didn't carry certain brands simply because those brands didn't move fast enough. Finally, after about six months sleuthing, a list of 110 distillery addresses in Scotland was put together and we wrote directly to them, asking:

a) do you export? (and we knew very well they did)
b) what is your FOB price to a Canadian liquor
   control board?
c) what is your FAX number?
d) would you quote to us for Private Stock Orders?

Much to our deep chagrin only ten replies were received! Two of the replies said that they were not interested, sixty came back "Not known at this address," and the others were puzzled. They said that they already had agents in Canada and why couldn't we go through them? Well, we would dearly love to, if we could only find out who they were. However, that would represent an extra step in our ordering process in any case, and here we were trying to speed things up.

The position of the agent was interesting. The distillery is rightfully protective of the agency, particularly if the agent is doing a good job. The role of **An Quaich** was, of course, immediately questioned. Then the agent was also wondering what **An Quaich** was doing, possibly thinking of commissions going down the drain. In this respect, there might have been some grounds for concern. It must be understood that the malt Scotch whisky revenues for any agent are minuscule at best because that agent represents only one or two brands. Though the volume of malt Scotch whisky sales might be very small (commissions are about $1.00 per bottle) compared to his or her inventory of wines, beers, liqueurs and other spirits including Scotch (the blended variety), those small sales represent the contact with the distilleries and distributors for those other spirits. However, here was an organization whose *only* interest was not just one or two brands of malt Scotch whisky, but the entire range of brands. Would the distilleries request **An Quaich** to undertake blends also? That thought alone would now give legitimate cause for ulcers. It took us a long time to realize that in some quarters we were regarded as a serious competitor. It was frustrating because **An Quaich** was not and is not interested in commissions - and we posed no threat because, being obliged to go through the liquor board, the commission on any sales made to **An Quaich** would automatically go to the official agent.

For example, one large distillery that officially represents five brands openly admits it imports only one of them because the others don't sell fast enough. The one brand they do import, they promote only at Christmas time! Yet **An Quaich** cannot order, even through that distillery, because they do not have the time nor are the orders big enough. It is realized that at the best of times, the economics of the industry is almost a game of Russian roulette. In bad economic times, it is worse. But is it not precisely at this time that the long-range potential should be considered? Is it not at this time, or any time for that matter, that altruistic promoters should be courted or at least encouraged? Indeed, there are many indications that the whole liquor control scenario across Canada needs to be examined.

As a result of further inquiries and reading of reports it became apparent that the big three in Scotland (Allied Lyons, Guinness, and United Distillers Group) had serious economic and projection problems with equally serious repercussions on small enterprises supplying blenders. Many distilleries, assured of a blend market, were quite happy with the *status quo.*

Is it at all possible then to get any brand, any time, even when buying a whole case? The answer is no. More frustrations? You bet. In many of our travels across Canada, it was noted that liquor stores in different provinces sold different brands. We got the bright idea that we could purchase from those sources, like an east-west free trade. After some inquiries we were told that, sure enough, we could proceed by way of domestic imports. But alas - our joy was short-lived.

An Quaich priced a bottle of Dalmore brought in from Scotland through the LCBO. The cost (at that time) was $34.00. The same bottle in Calgary was $32.00. Fair enough - there is no provincial sales tax in Alberta (at this writing). When that bottle was brought in to Ontario (that is called a "domestic import") the cost to the consumer was $43.00. No, it was not the freight. That came to a measly $1.25 per bottle. Though the LCBO got a discount from Alberta, the LCBO then put on its own mark-up and then the sales tax. Within our own country!

More frustration? Hang on, we're not through. We were so fascinated by the costing of domestic imports that we looked into the pricing structure of a regular import. No wonder liquor tax is considered a sin tax. Such taxation is indeed a sin and with the GST there is more to come. Here is a modest example:

Tullibardine dockside FO (12 x 750ml)	**B £29.96 or $ 66.22**
Duty	**39.93**
Federal Sales tax 19%	**19.98**
Freight to Glasgow	**4.00**
Liquor Board MARK-UP 120%	**156.03**
Levy	**2.88**
Environmental Tax	**53.52**
Provincial sales tax 12%	**41.11**

The total is $383.67 per case of twelve bottles or $31.97 each on a bottle of spirits that originally cost $5.52 (including all production costs and profit). If the 120% is indeed a mark-up and not a tax, then the government in question should be ashamed for allowing what cannot be anything else but excess profits. If it is a tax, then it should stay within the industry for better education and abuse prevention programs.

Many will say that liquor is a drug (that statement is open to debate because some very respected authorities consider it a food - as a carbohydrate), that nobody really needs it to live, so why not tax this super luxury item - just like cigarettes. My position is that liquor is not as dangerous as cigarettes, but that is another matter entirely. I do find it hard to discuss the necessity of liquor at times, but no product should suffer such mark-ups particularly when attendant services are admittedly wanting. Furthermore, good liquor produces many benefits. And why not disclose once in a while the ultimate destination of such profits? There are a lot of other luxury items out there that suffer only the ordinary taxes.

So, where does that leave us? The survival of societies like ours depends on their ability to provide a service. It is difficult to do so when there are that many limitations, handicaps and hurdles in our way. But we are determined. We are so convinced about the quality and the benefits of malt Scotch whisky (always in moderation) that we will not, we cannot, sit back and do nothing. We would like to help agents spread the goods and in the process help ourselves. In this respect **An Quaich** has only one goal in mind - to improve and expand the range of brands available to the consumer. One way would be by selling to bars, cafés, hotels, restaurants, clubs, members and other outlets. However, as a society we can only sell to our members. In fact we do not sell. We purchase on their behalf. Only as designated representatives of distributors or distillers would we be able to sell to licensed outlets. We have sought this designation from Scottish principals, but you already know the reaction. Then why all this persistence on our part?

We are interested in acquiring the broadest possible range of brands for our members and being able, eventually, to promote malt Scotch whisky as a table drink. What's in it for **An Quaich** then? Certainly not the commissions as mentioned before. We are motivated by fun, for one thing, and a much stronger purchasing power. Lest anybody get the idea, **An Quaich** is not entirely altruistic; we are also interested in income and profits. Growth of membership, writings and seminars would be ample for our needs. But do others in the industry see it in that light? It would not appear so, though some progress is being made, particularly among the agents. There is still the appearance of a "negative cooperation" though that also seems to be dissipating.

Though all of the above may sound discouraging, it has been anything but. Frustrating, yes, but discouraging, no. If anything, it has provided the incentive to pursue our goals. And here is another one.

Lastly and certainly not least, **An Quaich** is most interested in free trade. No, not the north-south variety, but east-west between the provinces. There is an adage to the effect that charity begins at home, and another that says that we should practise what we preach. Oh, that the federal and provincial politicians could at least give the impression of being less self-serving and really turn what talents they have towards good interprovincial programs and administration!

As the sun sets quietly behind the cnoc and a gentle breeze wafts over the waters, we deftly guide our good ship **An Quaich** into safe harbour, ready to head out to sea another day when we will confront those elements that are ignorant or unmindful of the uisge beatha. All cannot be said in one breath and many chapters yet remain unwritten. But ours is not to be silent and unsilent we shall be, trusting implicitly that you, good friend, will pursue in your own way the goals of **An Quaich.**

CHAPTER 16
THE ORIGINS

Before getting into the details of origins, I must caution the reader that the comments and evaluations that follow do not cover the whole gamut of malt Scotch whiskies. I have not explored all the brands, nor even every uisgage within a brand. For example, Glenfarclas has uisgages of eight, twelve, fifteen, twenty-one and twenty-five years and some in different strengths of alcohol by volume. I must be honest and say that, because of price, I have stayed with the eight and twelve year olds whenever possible. You can use another rule of thumb, however: the older the uisgage, the smoother and fuller the malt will be and unless it is aged in a sherry cask (even then) you should approach the first shot with tremendous respect and a few drops of water.

Now, discussing the origins of malt Scotch whisky is an area where there is quite a bit of controversy. I have yet to read two books that will give the exact same descriptions or use the same terms to indentify the location of malt Scotch whiskies. In most cases too many areas are mentioned and the names simply do not register. For example, the Lothian region produces exclusively Lowland malt and though they may have a bit more body than all the others, the distinction is very fine indeed. For our purposes, I have set out a list below of all the known brands available in Canada via the private stock order route or otherwise, though the availability can change overnight. The list is set up into four major areas that, in my opinion, present common taste characteristics. Some of these areas are further broken down along accepted lines for those that want to be choosy. The comments for each brand follow our tasting order of colour, legs, attack, presence, persistence, body, bite, smoke, peat and aftertaste.

THE ISLAND MALTS: this does not mean only the Islay (eye-ler) malts but all others coming from islands as such. Islays are from Islay specifically and are often mistaken as "the" Island malts.

There are other "island" malts coming, of course, from other Islands such as Talisker from Skye. I find that all of the Islay as well as the other island malts have a common characteristic which, however, varies to a considerable degree. These generally do well with crustaceans, strong fish, and strong, gamey meats. Here they are:

Orkney:
Highland Park - reddish tint, good legs, gentle strength that stays, full-bodied, delicate, slightly smoky and iodoform with a lingering, flowery aftertaste (probably due to the pinch of heather at malting). Food: save this one for an after-dinner drink or with a tart dessert. A dash of water will bring out the delicate aroma.

Islay:
Ardbeg - medium amber, good legs, medium strength that stays. Full body on the sharp side, medium smoke, little peat, short but full aftertaste. Food: salmon steak and slightly smoked cod, but NOT herring.

Bowmore - slightly darker than medium, medium legs, light, present and persistent. Slighter body on the delicate and smooth side of smoke. Light aftertaste. Food: plain white fish. The two will enhance each other. A good light after-dinner drink.

Bruichladdich - yellowish, fair legs, gentle and dissipating presence. Slighter body, rounded and on the rich side with a trace of peat. Good aftertaste. Food: snails, oysters. Some gamey birds like pheasant.

Bunnahabhain - dark amber, fair legs, gentle and mildly staying presence. Good body, gentle and very well-balanced for an Islay. Long smooth aftertaste. The only all purpose or "ordinaire" Islay. Food: anything not sweet. Superb with suet pudding.

Isle of Jura - light amber, medium legs, warm authoritative presence. Medium bodied, smooth and mellow, well-balanced. Short and sweet aftertaste. Food: mutual enhancement with light fish like trout and smelts.

Lagavulin - dark amber, heavy legs, sharp, very present and persistent. Full-bodied, heavy but well-balanced. Lingering aftertaste, smooths out. Food: anything gamey and strong like smoked herring, kippers and venison. Good with the hot and sharp steak tartar.

Laphroig - dark amber, very good legs. Sharp, present and persistent. Full-bodied, round, some smoke but un-balanced towards peat and iodoform. Long, heavy aftertaste. Food: does not enhance or balance too well. Best with light tangy meats or with potpourri.

Tobermory - medium amber, good legs. Gentle but persistent presence. Medium body, round, smooth and mellow with excellent balance. Smooth aftertaste. Food: excellent with a medium cheese like Bel Paese and light meats. Best with shrimp, crab and lobster.

Skye:

Talisker - light amber but good legs. Sharp, persistent presence. Full-bodied, round and slightly smoky but unbalanced towards the peat. Long, aromatic aftertaste. Food: THE companion for the traditional steak tartar and other tangy but not gamey meats.

Outer Hebrides:

Poit Dhubh - this is a special vatted malt bottled on Skye for the Gaelic-speaking people of the Hebrides. Heavy amber in colour with medium to heavy legs. The attack is gentle and the presence is only moderately persistent. Good round and well-balanced body with a moderate aftertaste. Food: will go very well with anything from soup to nuts. The dilution is the secret of its marriage to the dish offered.

THE LOWLAND MALTS: these are the malts that geographically come from an area south of an imaginary line drawn from Dundee to the northeast to Greenoch just west of Glasgow. As mentioned before, each malt has its own characteristics and some differ greatly although distilled only yards from each other as in the case of Mortlach and THE Glenlivet, but Lowland malt Scotch whiskies do have common characteristics in that they are lighter in colour, have runnier legs than the norm, are lighter to the taste and have a better than average staying power. These are by far the better malts to have at the dinner table for general purposes in that they should be diluted only slightly if at all, and they mix well with any dish other than those with very specific flavours or aromas. It may be confusing to the reader to find that the same region may be named when giving the origin of Lowland malts and again when giving the origin of Highland malts. The answer is that these regions straddle the Highland/Lowland line and therefore have northern and southern sectors. For this reason, particular attention should be paid to the taste commentary. The regions named swing from west to east on the map and head north. Lastly, a short note on each of the sub-regions in this area would be in order so that the reader might get a better appreciation of subtle differences and nomenclature. It should also be noted that two well-known names are not discussed at length. The first is Inverleven and the reason is that it is not readily available as a bottled malt. The second is Ladyburn and the reason here is that this most excellent Lowland malt is no longer available. It is now a collector's item.

Strathclyde: the delta and valley of the river Clyde on the west coast between Glasgow and Greenoch.

Auchentoshan - very pale amber and light legs, gentle but marked presence dissipating rather quickly. This may be due to its triple distillation. Light body and mellow. Very well-balanced with a delicate and noted aftertaste. This one is marked for the ladies, though in this day and age one hesitates to associate things delicate with the feminine gender. Food: excellent balance or enhancement with light fowl and veal.

Glen Scotia - darker amber than one would expect of a Lowland malt. Also heavier legs. Has a slightly sharp and lingering presence. Full bodied for a Lowland but traditionally mellow and sweet peat flavour. The aftertaste is long and delicate. An uncharacteristic Lowland. Food: one of the better ones with medium white fish. Careful of the oily ones or the dry and flaky. Excellent with trout. Also goes well with a medium cheese like Brick and particularly Oka.

Littlemill - slightly darker than average and "leggy" for a Lowland malt. Gentle to the nose but very evident. Light and mellow body that is well balanced. Smooth lingering aftertaste. This is a "heavy" Lowland. Food: this excellent malt will enhance the meaty potpourri dishes. It would be wasted on fish. It's a classic with a fancy type of middle cheese like a St. Paulin or La Grappe which is a kirsch cheese of all things. Try this one with suet pudding!

Springbank - very light with runny legs. Delicate persistence. Full but not heavy body, very well-balanced. Delicate, lingering aftertaste. Definitely one for the ladies! Food: any dish would be likely to overshadow this fine malt. Should be drunk by itself. If you must, then it will enhance a delicately seasoned veal with a light neutral sauce.

Wigton: in the southwest of the Lowlands. If the Lowland malts are supposed to mature more quickly, then the "uisgage" of this one and only malt could be gauged in days and not years. Yet it's a dandy in its own right.

Bladnoch - light amber and light legs. Gentle and airy to the nose. Light body and delicate taste. Very smooth and well-balanced. Sweet and light aftertaste. Food: Better keep this one as an aperitif.

Ladyburn - this is a medium of everything and blends with foods accordingly. From Ayr to the northwest of Wigton.

Lothian: we now go back south-east of Edinburgh. Though we are getting close to the sea we find that most east coast malts retain inland characteristics, probably because the prevailing westerly winds would have lost any "sea air" (if indeed that would have anything to do with the flavour of the one brand presently available for export).

Glenkinchie - pale amber and light legs. Gentle nose and persistence dissipates rather quickly though marked. Light, very well-balanced body with a heavier than expected aftertaste. Food: Mostly a light after-dinner drink but goes well with pastry desserts - one of the few with that faculty!

THE HIGHLAND MALTS: sorting out the Highland malts is a real dog's breakfast. Again, most books do not bother giving the reader an idea of where the regions quoted are situated. Not only does this make it difficult to locate the brands but also more difficult to appreciate the possible reasons why the groupings do taste different. I have once more identified the regions by broad characteristics and I must say that generally most authorities agree on these groupings though the names might be different. For example, some authors still identify Campbeltown malts. There are only two left and they are the Glen Scotia and Rosebank. Because of their taste and general location, however, they fit very nicely in the Strathclyde group of Lowlands.

This brings me to the divisions of the Highland malts. I have found that all malt Scotch whiskies along the Caledonian Canal have a good number of common characteristics. Now the Caledonian Canal stretches from the Firth of Lorne (between the islands of Jura and Mull on the west coast), travelling northeasterly to Inverness and along the shores of the Moray Firth to Brora, home of the Dalmore. These I call the Caledonian or Western Highlands. Moving in an easterly direction towards Dundee along the valley of the river Tay is, of course, the Tayside region. Virtually all else to the north is considered the Grampian region.

Now, about the taste. The Caledonians have slightly heavier legs than the Lowlands and consequently more body. They are generally well-balanced but if anything they might have a slightly smoky but smooth characteristic. Inasmuch as the Island malts generally have the heaviest legs, the second heaviest generally belong to the Grampians. These malts will also have the greatest range of variations within the group and this is not surprising, considering the number of brands with which to contend. It is in this group that we find more brands aged in sherry casks, as well as vatted malts, than the "pure" Highland malt. The vatted is simply a mixture of one batch of single malt with another of the same brand. These may still legally be termed "pure" but when you see on the label just the words "Highland malt" without the other words "pure" or "single," then the chances are you almost assuredly have a mixture of several batches or brands of single malt. Some mistake these to be "double" malts, on the basis, I suppose, that if there are single malts, there must be doubles. I believe that the double may come from the idea of the mixture or the number of distillations, Auchentoshan, for example, being triple distilled.

However, as we have many, many brands to discuss here, it may be best to single out their characteristics as we go. Finally, there are the true Highland malts. These are a bit darker than the Grampians but it really takes an expert's eye to catch the subtle hue. Another factor to consider is that these Highlanders are very close to the "Caledonians" geographically and in character.

Caledonians:

Balblair - pale amber and surprisingly runny legs. Gentle and light to the nose. Medium and smooth body that is well-balanced. Light aftertaste. Food: this malt is a stranger to its brethren as is Mortlach in its region. This is the lightweight of the Caledonian gang. Keep it as an after-dinner drink. It has a clean and refreshing taste. Though very different than Glengoyne, this one chilled holds a very pleasant surprise.

Ben Wyvis - this is another pale and runny renegade. There was a special bottling which may never be repeated and this is the sad part of Scottish distilling policies. They can't make up their minds. The very gentle presence is the only indication that it ages in sherry casks. Medium, rich, smooth and sweet body. The sweet aftertaste betrays the peat. Food: another lightweight to save for the fireplace. Don't chill this one. If anything, warm it up slightly.

Clynelish - slightly darker than medium and good legs. Round and persistent to the nose. Moderately full and sweet body with a trace of iodine coming through the peat. The moderately lasting aftertaste shows more of the iodine. Food: definitely a companion for venison and will enhance lobster and scallops. Will overpower shrimp and crab.

Dalmore - rich amber and excellent legs. Very round and persistent. Full and mellow with a trace of peat. Exceptional aftertaste. Food: do you shovel dirt with a silver spade? Dalmore is the after-dinner drink par excellence but if you must, then serve slightly diluted (with tears) and with nothing but the best standing rib.

Glen Albyn - medium amber and medium legs. Gentle and slightly airy for a Caledonian. Medium well-balanced body with attendant aftertaste. Food: this is the Caledonian equivalent of the Lowland's Deanston. Will go well with anything but soft cheese. Keep in mind the fuller body than Deanston and therefore its propensity to heavier foods - cuts the rich ones nicely.

Glen Mohr - for once two distilleries side by side produce almost the same thing. The only difference is that Glen Mohr is slightly sweeter with a nice peaty aftertaste. Food: the comments about Glen Albyn apply but watch the sweetness. This one will not cut well with rich foods - or heavy ones for that matter.

Glenmorangie - on the pale side of medium but with good legs. Slightly sharp and airy nose. Body on the light side with sweet peat. Medium lasting aftertaste allows a trace of smoke to come through. Food: this one is very interesting as an aperitif in preparation for a meal of strong fowl.

Oban - dark amber with excellent legs. Sharp and persistent. The body is on the full side of medium. A smooth smoke is gently prodded with a sweet peat which comes out in a gentle, persistent aftertaste. Food: very good as an aperitif to shellfish and with pastry. No cheese please.

Ord - medium amber with slightly heavy legs. Round and persistent to the nose. Medium body, smooth but with a slightly musty peat that comes out in a rather quickly dissipating aftertaste. It is better known as Glenordie. Food: probably best as a cold weather aperitif.

Pulteney - from the northernmost distillery on the mainland it is dark with good legs. Sharp with a heavy persistence. Full body, smooth and mellow. A lingering aftertaste reveals a subtle peatiness. Food: it goes well with light fish such as trout and salmon depending on the preparation.

Sheep Dip - not as bad as the name implies. This is another vatted malt and, like virtually all "vats," it is darker than usual, smoother and with good legs. The body is round and well-balanced with an average aftertaste. Food: it also will go well with just about anything.

Highland: this is where I will be taken to task on the selection of my regions. Indeed, some of the brands in the Caledonian category are usually found in the Highland classification. By the same token, virtually all of the Grampians could also be classified as Highland. I can only repeat what I have said before, that I have used a classification as close to the traditional ones as I could but in geographical groups that I found had more common characteristics. At the risk of repeating myself, I found that the Caledonians had more of a peaty characteristic than any of the others. We all now know about the iodoforme or medicinal characteristic of the Islay malts and the gentle lightness of the Lowlands. Now we move from the peat through an area that is slightly more balanced towards the Grampians. There are only a few in my Highland group.

Dalwhinnie - pale amber with medium legs. Sharpish sting with a strong and persistent presence. Full body and delicate bite, quite smooth and sweet. Well-balanced with a mellow, lingering aftertaste. Food: this would be primarily a pre-dinner drink in the same class as a medium sherry. Somewhat delicate for cheeses and a bit classy for the table. However, it would be excellent with roast beef, cipaille, steak and kidney pie, and light fowl.

Tomatin - pale amber but with surprisingly heavy legs. Light with medium but persistent presence. Medium body that is delicate, smooth and sweet. There is a lingering, mellow aftertaste. Food: this one will go with anything. It is the Deanston of the Highlands. Diluted about ten percent it would contribute nicely to any dish with a rolled oats base.

Grampian: many authorities combine all that is east of the Caledonian Canal and north of the Greenoch-Dundee line as "Grampian." This is simplistic. Not that I want to complicate matters but I feel that I must follow the principle of "taste demarcation," much as I have done for the Caledonian designation. In that respect, the next region is Speyside. It normally should cover only the valley of the Spey, but in effect goes from the Findhorn River east to the North Sea, north of the river Tay. The region to the southeast of Speyside would, of course, be Tayside. Then coming back west from the Edinburgh-Dundee line is the Central Region. It should be noted that the term "highlands" for Scotland is given a number of meanings such as "to the north" or "mountains" or again the high ground in terms of above sea level. The true Highlands encompassing all three aspects have been dealt with above. The Grampian region is a special region because of those subtle differences in tastes mentioned before. This no doubt makes the purist happy. Uisgage for uisgage, these are a bit mellower than the true Highland malt. To separate them according to these sub-regions is quite useful if only because few of the books I have read agree on the categorization. Again, I have gone on my own, on a limb if you wish, but I have made what I believe to be the most accurate compilation from all sources. A detailed Map File follows this chapter to substantiate my claim.

Speyside:

Aberlour - typical medium Grampian amber with equally medium legs. Medium-light to the nose with good persistent presence. A rather full body with some bite but a smooth sweet taste. There is a lingering aftertaste. Food: good with custards and sweet desserts but this brand is best as an after-dinner drink.

Auchriosk - darker amber with the heavier legs that go with malt matured in sherry casks. Very delicate with medium presence. The body is relatively full and well-rounded. Very smooth and sweet. The aftertaste is not as lingering as one would want it to be. Food: Sweet fruit desserts. Do keep this one as a pousse-café.

Aultmore - medium amber and medium legs. The nose is on the delicate side with a persistent medium presence. It is full, delicate, mellow and smooth but with a short aftertaste. Food: good with heavy fowl and any of the potpourri combinations.

Balvenie - medium amber but heavier than usual legs. Very delicate nose with a medium but persistent presence. Full-bodied, rounded, smooth and sweet. Excellent aftertaste that lingers. Food: Light meats and desserts; this is an ideal after-dinner drink.

Benriach- pale amber and light legs. Sharpish nose with light and fleeting presence. Light, delicate pungency of peat with little aftertaste. Food: Excellent with cipaille, potpourri, and anything else. This is the versatile "Deanston" of the Highlands.

Benromach - a twin for Benriach without the peat. Berry's Pure Malt: slightly darker amber than expected even of a sherry cask aging, medium legs. The nose is on the sharp side, noticeable presence and persistence. Full and blunt but smooth, mellow and well-balanced. Good lingering aftertaste. Food: light creamy desserts. Good strong pousse-café.

Berry's Pure Malt - slightly darker amber than expected even of a sherry cask aging, medium legs. The nose is on the sharp side, noticeable presence and persistence. Full and blunt but smooth, mellow and well balanced. Good lingering aftertaste. Food: light creamy desserts. Good strong pousse café.

Caperdonich - medium-light coloured, runny legs. Light and fleeting to the nose. Round, light-bodied and well-balanced. Good after-dinner drink. Food: this is one of the rare malts that can be labelled as dry. Excellent with soups and desserts.

Cardhu - light coloured but with good legs. Marked sting with a strong and persistent presence. Full yet delicate body, very well-balanced and clean with a good persistent aftertaste. Food: a very good after-dinner drink but probably best with haggis and all oat and meal dishes. Has few peers if any in this area.

Craigellachie - medium amber and light legs for a Grampian. Nose is medium sting with medium and volatile presence. Light-bodied, delicate with the balance favouring an aromatic smoke. Good aftertaste. One of the good light after-dinner drinks. Food: Very good with fish based potpourri and heavy meats.

Cragganmore - medium amber with excellent legs. Medium sting to the nose with strong and persistent presence. Full, well-rounded body and very well-balanced with good aftertaste. A classic Grampian. Good after-dinner drink. Food: goes well with any food. One of the most versatile Highland malts. With food it should be cut ten to fifteen percent.

Dufftown - medium amber with good legs. Slightly sharp on the nose with a medium and persistent presence. Full and rounded body with a delicate, smooth taste. Has a moderately lingering and mellow aftertaste. Slightly mellower than the Dalwhinnie, it also is an excellent pre-dinner drink. Food: good with light puddings but is best as an aperitif.

Fettercairn - rather dark golden colour and medium legs. Light to the nose with a medium but persistent presence. Full and well-rounded body, smooth with a sweet peatiness. Mellow, lingering aftertaste. Another excellent after-dinner drink. Food: could balance off tart desserts very well.

Glenallachie - medium-golden colour and medium legs. Light to the nose with a medium and fleeting presence. Medium and delicate body that is well-balanced. The aftertaste is mellow but fleeting. Food: this is an excellent Grampian malt with considerable versatility. Will complement any dish.

Glenburgie - medium amber and slightly runny legs. Much the same as the Glenallachie.

Glendronach - (traditional - oak cask) medium amber and very good legs. Marked nose with a good and persistent presence. The body is full and round. Well-balanced with a strong but rich aftertaste. This is a heavy-duty, all round brand. Food: exceptional with any dish. The degree of dilution is the secret to this one.

Glendronach - (sherry cask) very dark amber and heavy legs. Sharp nose with a strong and persistent presence. Full and delicate body, very well-balanced with a mellow and lingering aftertaste. An after-dinner drink par excellence. Food: you wouldn't dare! In fact any food would spoil this gem. It is, in my opinion, one of the three after-dinner dinner classics. Balvenie was one of the other two - though lighter.

Glendullan - medium golden colour with medium legs. Light sting with a medium presence moderately persistent. Good but strong body, well- balanced and smooth. It has a nutty, lingering taste making it a good after-dinner drink. Food: mixes well with any meat (beef) dish. A good general purpose malt when diluted ten percent.

Glen Elgin - medium amber with rather good legs suggesting sherry cask aging. Moderate sting with a medium presence moderately persistent. Full body with moderate bite, it is smooth accentuated towards the sweet with a lingering aftertaste. Food: because it has a general aromatic character that comes through, it is better as an after- dinner drink than with food.

Glenesk - a twin to Glen Elgin in every respect but with more body.

Glenfarclas - dark amber with very good legs. Sharp to the nose but with a moderate presence quite persistent. Full-bodied and delicate. Very well-balanced with a lingering aftertaste. Food: Obviously a sherry cask aged malt and therefore a natural after-dinner drink. Good with strong, wild meats. The 105 must be diluted if you want to die a natural death!

Glenfiddich - Pale golden colour with medium legs. Sharp nose with moderate but persistent presence. Full-bodied with some bite but well-balanced. A dry lingering aftertaste. A natural aperitif. Food: would go well with anything at all. This is not an uisgage (no age declared at this writing) and is best as an aperitif.

Glen Garioch - pale amber colour but lighter legs than expected. Light sting with good and persistent presence. Full and delicate body with a slightly sweet peatiness. Lingering aftertaste. Food: good with light fish but preferable as an after-dinner drink.

Glen Grant - pale amber with good legs. Medium sting with similar presence and persistence. Full yet delicate body, smooth with a peaty sweetness. Persistent aftertaste. Excellent after-dinner drink. Food: light meats and desserts.

Glenleven - another lost child mentioned only by Jackson. This is a vatted brand comprised of six malts. Its colour is light to medium amber with medium to slow legs. The attack and presence are definite but dissipate quickly. It has a light, well-balanced body with a lingering, smooth aftertaste. Food: No. This is a light malt Scotch that is best as an aperitif or a pousse-café.

Glenlivet (THE) - medium amber with good legs. Sharp nose with moderate but persistent presence. Full-bodied with some bite but well-balanced. Lingering aftertaste. A natural aperitif or after- dinner drink. Slightly heavier than Glenfiddich. Food: would go well with anything but best kept as aperitif or after-dinner.

Glen Moray - pale amber with good but light legs. Medium nose, presence and persistence. Medium-bodied, delicate, smooth with a slight musty peatiness. Its lightness makes it a natural as an aperitif. Food: will balance anything rather well. Should be only slightly diluted. Becomes an expensive proposition and therefore best kept as an aperitif.

Glenugie - medium amber with medium legs. Light nose with medium presence and persistence. Medium body, delicate, smooth with a slight musty sweetness. Food: excellent with any medium dessert.

Glenury-Royal - pale golden colour with light legs. Sharp nose with medium presence and persistence. Light-bodied, delicate, slightly unbalanced towards smoke. An excellent cold-weather, pre-dinner drink. Food: light fish dishes that need enhancing, but still best as a pre-dinner drink.

Inchgower - medium amber with good legs. Medium nose, presence and persistence. Good, round body with some bite but very good balance. Has a surprisingly lingering aftertaste. Food: will go well with anything but is exceptional as the pousse-café after a heavy meal.

Knockando - light golden colour with fine legs. Light nose with moderate presence and persistence. Round but not full body, delicate with the balance towards smoke. The aftertaste is nutty, mellow but on the short side. Good aperitif or after-dinner drink. Food: any dish with light spice.

Linkwood - medium amber with average legs. Sharpish nose with good and persistent presence. Light body with medium bite with a touch of smoke in the balance. Light smoky lingering aftertaste. A very versatile malt, excellent at any time. Food: excellent with any food. The results will depend on the dilution.

Macallan - dark amber and heavy legs. Medium nose with a definite and persistent presence. Full and round yet delicate. Very well-balanced with a very mellow and lingering aftertaste. This is the third of my classic trio. A superb after-dinner drink. Food: Noooo way. Never. I will disown you! And so would 99.99% of the connoisseur fraternity.

Milton-Duff - medium amber with medium legs. Medium nose with medium presence and persistence. However, it is full-bodied yet delicate. Smooth and sweet, it has a mellow lingering aftertaste. Very good all round. Food: will mix well with any food.

Mortlach - very pale colour, good legs. Light nose, medium but lingering presence. Round but not full body. Delicate and smooth with peaty mustiness. A good versatile light drink. Food: this number has only one place - with the glandular meats. Superb with kidneys, heart and liver.

Royal Lochnagar - (sometimes called simply Lochnagar) medium amber with good legs. Medium nose with a definite but only medium persistence. Good body, delicate and smooth with a trace of nutty mustiness. Good but not persistent aftertaste. Food: excellent with all meats and light puddings.

Strathconon - medium golden colour and good legs. Sharpish nose with a definite but not persistent presence. Good body with a sharpish bite and a trace of smoke. Light smoky but lingering aftertaste. A very good aperitif. Food: excellent with light fish.

Strathisla - dark amber and good legs. Moderate nose with a very definite and persistent presence. Very full and round body yet delicate. Very well-balanced. Has a mellow and lingering aftertaste. Food: Not really.

Tamdhu - medium amber and good legs. Sharp nose with a definite and persistent presence. Full yet delicate body. Very well-balanced and mellow. Light lingering aftertaste. Best as aperitif or after-dinner drink. Food: this brand of malt is very versatile. Will go well with any food.

Tamnavulin - very light golden colour. Runny legs. Light nose with an indefinite presence and little persistence. Light-bodied and very well balanced. Mellow and surprisingly lingering aftertaste. Chilled, this is a summertime aperitif par excellence. Food: because of its light-ness, this malt would go well with any-thing. This might be expensive because to dilute it at all means a loss of charac-ter.

Tomintoul - medium amber with average legs. Light nose with medium presence and persistence. Light but round body, smooth and well-balanced. Lingering mellow aftertaste. Food: Although best as a light after-dinner drink, will go well with any beef.

Tayside:

Blair Athol - medium amber and medium legs. Sharpish nose on the strong and persistent side. Full-bodied and slightly rounded, smooth taste. Slightly smoky with only a slight aftertaste. Food: good with any meat that has marked flavour. Adequate, but not the best after-dinner drink.

Edradour - medium amber with considerable legs. The nose is on the sharp side with a medium presence and persistence. The body is rather full and quite round. The balance swings towards a sweet mustiness of peat giving a mellow and lasting aftertaste. Please keep this as the mellow after-dinner drink. Food: can be used with anything - but shouldn't. If you must, then concentrate on light beef meats and dark meats of domestic fowl. No game please.

Glenforres - only Cooper and Jackson mention this vatted relative of Edradour. The label states "12 years old" indicating that the youngest component is of that uisgage. It is pale gold in colour with rather runny legs. The attack is light and smooth and the little presence there is dissipates quickly. The body is light, smooth and well-balanced with a moderately lasting smooth aftertaste. Food: will go well with anything, diluted no more than five percent.

Glen Turret - golden colour with very good legs. Medium nose but a good persistent presence. Full-bodied, delicate, smooth and well- balanced. Moderately persistent aftertaste. Excellent all round drink best as aperitif or after-dinner. Food: meats if you must. It is delicate to the point that dilution is not recommended. It is therefore a bit strong for food - and expensive.

Tullibardine - medium amber with average legs. Light nose but a definite and persistent presence. Full body that is well-balanced. Has a slightly musty and lingering aftertaste. Very nice aperitif or after-dinner drink. Food: goes well with glandular meats and medium fish. Quite versatile.

Central: means what it says. This region lies roughly between Glasgow and Edinburgh and straddles the imaginary Greenoch-Dundee line dividing the Lowlands from the Highlands, most of it lying south. The following malts will have more body and persistence than their traditional Lowland cousins though they are very closely related. These will be an excellent match for most basic foods. Note that Deanston is sometimes considered as a Tayside malt. However, it is distilled quite a distance from that area and the more accurate location is very much Central.

Deanston - slightly darker golden-amber with good legs. Gentle and airy, dissipating rather quickly. Good medium body and well-balanced. Mellow and surprisingly persistent aftertaste. Food: This is the one we have been waiting for. This is the *vin ordinaire* of the malts. You can't go wrong with this one with any dish. The trick here is to know when not to dilute it and when you do, just how much. Deanston has that rare quality of being able to meld with any food, yet keep just enough strength to enhance or balance.

Glengoyne - dark amber yet not aged in sherry casks. Good legs. Round and persistent. Medium, mellow body with a very delicate and persistent aftertaste. This one is different to all the Lowlands. It sits right on the Dundee-Greenoch line and is usually classified as a Highland malt. The decision to put it with the Lowlands is mine alone and based on the fact that it has too many of the Lowland characteristics to be a Highland in spite of its equally many exceptions. Food: Preferably kept as an after-dinner drink and this one is a real dream of a dram when chilled. Of any food-stuff, Glengoyne would probably be best with a soft cheese like Camembert.

Rosebank: light amber and light legs. Sharpish and persistent. Light and very well-balanced body. Somewhat sweet and wispy aftertaste. Food: Another excellent all-purpose food companion though not as versatile as Deanston. It is a bit heavier and sits best with meats. Goes well with hard, strong old cheddars. Also good as an aperitif. This malt is triple distilled as is the Auchentoshan.

This is the list that I have at this writing. There are many more brands that I have not evaluated or that I have left out either because they no longer exist or because they are not readily available. By the same token, there are some that I have listed which may disappear from the market or may become quite difficult to obtain, even through **An Quaich**! My heart goes out to you, because when you have latched on to a combination of food and drink, and the drink is then taken off the market because it does not produce enough money, frustration knows no bounds. I know.

The table that follows should be quite useful to you in checking selections against what you plan to serve at the table.

Beannachd leibh agus slainte mhath! Goodbye and to your good health!

FOOD CAMPATIBILITY CHART (Page One)

The number's under each heading indicate the degree of propriety on a scale of 1 to 3, the highest being the best.

	Aperitif	Meat							Fish				Potpourri	Birds			Cheese			Desserts			Pousse Cafe
	BDD	Lamb	Pork	Beef	Veal	Glan	Stew	Spec	Crus	White	Med	Oily	PP	Dry	Moist	Ganey	Hard	Med	Soft	Pies	Pudd	Misc	PC
THE ISLAND MALTS:																							
Ardbeg	1	-	1	-	-	-	-	-	2	-	-	3	-	-	-	-	-	-	-	-	-	-	1
Bowmore	3	1	1	-	-	-	-	2	1	-	-	-	-	-	-	3	-	-	-	-	-	-	3
Bruichladdich	1	-	-	-	-	-	-	1	3	-	-	-	-	-	3	-	-	2	-	-	-	-	1
Bunnahabhain	2	2	2	2	2	1	-	2	1	1	-	-	2	-	-	-	3	-	-	-	3	-	3
Highland Park	2	-	-	-	-	1	1	-	2	2	-	-	-	-	1	-	1	-	-	1	-	-	3
Isle of Jura	1	1	1	-	-	-	-	-	2	3	-	-	-	-	-	-	-	-	-	1	3	-	1
Lagavulin	2	1	2	2	1	1	1	2	3	-	-	-	2	1	-	-	3	-	-	1	3	-	3
Laphroig	3	2	1	-	1	1	1	3	1	1	-	3	2	1	1	1	1	1	-	1	3	1	1
Poit Dhubh	2	1	1	1	1	1	1	-	-	1	-	1	1	1	1	-	3	1	-	-	1	-	3
Talisker	2	2	1	1	1	1	1	3	2	1	2	3	-	1	-	-	1	2	-	-	-	1	1
Tobermory	2	2	2	2	2	-	1	3	3	-	-	-	2	-	-	-	3	-	-	-	3	-	3
THE LOWLAND MALTS:																							
Auchentoshan(Strathclyde)	-	1	-	-	3	-	-	-	-	-	-	-	-	2	-	-	-	-	-	-	-	-	-
Bladnoch	3	-	-	-	-	-	-	-	-	-	-	-	-	-	-	-	-	-	-	-	-	-	-
Glenkinchle	-	-	-	-	-	-	-	-	-	-	-	-	-	-	-	-	3	-	-	3	-	-	-
Glenscotia (Strathclyde)	1	-	-	-	-	-	-	3	-	3	1	-	2	-	-	-	3	3	-	1	-	3	3
Littlemill (Strathclyde)	2	-	-	-	-	-	-	3	-	3	1	-	2	2	-	-	3	1	-	-	-	1	3
Ladyburn	1	1	1	1	1	1	1	1	-	1	1	-	1	2	1	1	1	1	-	1	3	2	1
Springbank (Strathclyde)	3	2	2	3	3	-	3	3	-	-	2	-	-	-	-	-	-	1	-	-	1	1	-
THE CALEDONIAN MALTS:																							
Balblair	-	-	-	-	-	-	-	-	-	-	-	-	-	-	-	-	-	-	-	-	-	-	3
Ben Wyvis	1	-	-	-	-	-	-	-	-	-	-	-	-	-	-	-	-	-	-	-	-	-	3
Clynelish	3	1	3	-	-	-	-	3	2	-	-	-	1	-	2	-	2	-	-	-	-	-	3
Dalmore	3	-	3	-	-	-	-	3	1	-	-	-	-	-	3	-	-	-	-	-	-	-	3
Glen Albyn	2	1	2	1	1	1	2	1	1	2	1	-	1	1	-	1	1	-	-	-	1	-	-
Glen Mhor	2	1	2	1	1	1	2	2	1	1	1	-	1	1	-	1	1	-	-	-	-	-	-
Glenmorangie	3	-	3	-	-	-	-	-	2	1	1	-	1	1	1	2	-	-	-	1	-	-	3
Oban (Strathclyde)	3	-	-	-	-	-	-	-	-	-	-	-	-	-	2	1	2	-	-	2	-	-	-
Ord (Glenordie)	3	-	-	-	-	-	-	-	-	-	-	-	-	-	-	-	-	-	-	-	-	-	-
Pulteney	1	1	1	1	1	1	1	1	1	2	1	-	-	-	-	-	1	-	-	1	-	-	-
Sheep Dip	1	1	1	1	1	1	1	1	1	1	1	-	1	1	1	1	1	1	-	1	1	1	1

FOOD CAMPATIBILITY CHART (Page Two)

	Aperitif	Meat							Fish				Potpourri	Birds			Cheese			Desserts			Pousse Cafe
	BDO	Lamb	Pork	Beef	Veal	Glan	Stew	Spec	Crus	White	Med	Oily	PP	Dry	Moist	Ganey	Hard	Med	Soft	Pies	Pudd	Misc	PC
HIGHLAND MALTS:																							
Dalwhinnie	3	-	1	3	-	-	1	2	-	-	-	-	-	1	2	-	-	-	-	-	-	-	2
Tomatin	2	1	1	2	2	1	1	3	1	2	1	-	2	-	2	-	2	-	1	1	-	-	1
CENTRAL MALTS:																							
Deanston	2	1	2	2	2	1	2	1	-	1	-	-	2	2	2	1	2	-	-	2	1	1	1
Glengoyne	-	-	-	-	-	-	-	-	1	-	-	-	-	-	-	-	-	3	3	2	2	1	3
Rosebank	3	1	2	2	2	-	2	-	-	-	-	-	-	-	-	-	3	-	-	-	-	-	1
SPEYSIDE MALTS:																							
Aberlour	1	-	-	-	-	-	-	-	-	-	-	-	-	-	-	-	-	-	-	-	-	-	3
Auchriosk	-	-	-	1	-	-	-	-	-	-	-	-	-	-	-	1	-	-	-	-	-	2	3
Aultmore	1	-	1	1	-	-	-	2	-	-	-	-	3	-	-	3	-	1	-	-	-	1	1
Balvenie	2	-	-	-	3	-	-	-	3	-	-	-	-	-	-	3	-	2	3	-	1	-	3
Benriach	2	2	2	2	1	1	1	2	-	1	1	-	2	2	1	-	1	1	2	1	1	1	2
Benromach	2	1	1	2	1	1	1	2	-	1	1	-	2	2	1	-	1	1	2	1	2	2	1
Berry's Pure Malt	3	-	-	1	-	-	1	2	2	-	-	-	-	-	-	-	-	-	-	2	2	-	3
Caperdonich	1	-	-	1	-	-	-	-	-	-	-	1	-	-	-	-	1	-	-	-	2	2	2
Cardhu	2	-	-	1	-	-	3	-	1	-	-	-	3	-	-	-	-	-	-	-	1	-	2
Craigallachie	2	-	-	1	2	1	1	2	-	-	-	-	3	-	-	-	-	-	-	-	-	1	1
Cragganmore	3	-	1	2	-	-	2	1	-	-	-	-	2	-	1	-	2	1	-	-	-	1	3
Dufftoun	3	-	-	1	-	1	-	-	1	1	1	-	-	-	1	-	-	-	-	-	-	-	3
Fettercairn	-	-	-	-	-	-	-	-	-	-	-	1	-	-	-	-	-	-	-	2	-	1	1
Glenallachie	1	1	1	1	1	1	1	1	1	1	1	1	1	1	1	1	1	1	1	1	1	1	3
Glenburgie	1	1	1	1	1	1	1	1	1	1	1	-	1	1	1	1	1	1	1	1	1	1	2
Glendronach (original)	3	1	2	2	1	1	1	1	1	2	2	-	2	1	3	1	2	2	1	1	1	1	2
Glendronach (sherry)	3	1	1	1	-	-	2	2	-	2	2	-	2	-	-	-	-	-	-	1	3	2	3
Glendullan	-	-	-	3	2	-	-	-	-	-	-	2	1	-	-	-	1	-	-	-	-	-	2
Glen Elgin	1	-	-	-	-	-	-	-	1	-	-	1	1	-	1	-	-	-	-	-	-	-	2
Glenesk	1	-	-	1	1	1	-	-	-	-	-	-	-	-	-	-	1	-	-	-	-	-	3
Glenfarclas	3	2	2	2	1	1	1	1	1	1	-	2	2	1	1	1	1	1	-	1	1	1	2
Glenfiddich	2	1	1	1	1	1	2	1	1	1	1	2	2	1	1	1	1	1	-	1	1	1	3
Glen Garioch	1	-	-	1	-	-	2	1	-	2	1	1	-	-	-	-	-	1	-	-	-	-	1

FOOD CAMPATIBILITY CHART (Page Three)

	Aperitif	Meat							Fish				Potpourri			Birds			Cheese			Desserts			Pousse Cafe
	BID	Lamb	Pork	Beef	Veal	Glan	Stew	Spec	Crus	White	Med	Oily	PP	Dry	Moist	Dry	Moist	Gamey	Hard	Med	Soft	Pies	Pudd	Misc	PC
Glen Grant	1	-	-	1	3	-	-	1	-	1	-	1	1	1	-	-	1	-	-	1	-	2	2	2	2
Glenlivet (THE)	3	1	1	2	1	1	1	1	1	1	-	1	1	1	1	1	1	-	1	2	1	1	1	2	1
Glen Moray	3	1	1	2	1	1	2	1	1	1	2	-	1	1	1	1	1	-	1	1	1	1	1	1	3
Glenugie	1	-	1	1	1	-	-	1	-	1	-	-	1	1	1	1	1	-	-	1	1	3	3	3	1
Glenury-Royal	3	1	-	-	1	-	-	-	3	2	1	1	1	1	1	1	1	-	3	1	1	1	1	1	3
Inchgower	1	1	2	1	1	1	1	1	1	1	1	1	1	1	1	1	1	-	1	1	1	1	1	1	2
Knockando	2	1	1	1	1	1	1	1	1	1	1	-	3	1	1	2	1	-	1	1	1	1	1	1	3
Linkwood	2	1	2	1	1	1	2	2	1	1	1	-	2	1	2	1	1	-	3	2	1	1	1	1	3
Macallan	3	-	-	-	-	1	1	1	-	2	-	-	-	1	-	1	2	-	1	1	-	1	-	-	2
Milton-Duff	2	-	1	2	2	1	1	2	-	1	-	-	1	2	1	2	1	1	1	1	-	1	-	-	-
Mortlach	1	3	2	2	2	3	1	3	-	1	1	-	1	1	1	1	1	1	1	1	-	-	2	1	-
Royal Lochnagar	-	1	2	-	1	1	2	1	-	-	1	-	-	1	-	-	-	-	-	1	-	-	-	-	1
Strathconon	3	-	-	-	-	-	-	-	-	2	1	2	1	1	-	1	1	1	-	1	-	1	-	-	3
Strathisla	2	-	1	1	1	1	1	1	1	1	1	-	-	1	-	1	1	-	1	1	1	1	1	1	2
Tandhu	3	1	1	1	1	1	2	2	1	1	1	-	2	2	1	1	2	-	1	2	1	2	1	2	2
Tannavulin	2	-	2	2	2	2	2	2	1	2	2	-	2	2	1	2	2	2	2	2	1	2	2	2	3
Tomintoul	2	-	2	2	2	-	1	1	-	1	-	-	-	1	-	1	1	-	1	1	-	1	-	1	3
TAYSIDE MALTS:																									
Blair Athol	-	2	-	-	-	-	-	1	-	-	1	-	-	1	1	-	1	1	-	1	-	1	-	-	3
Edradour	-	1	-	-	-	-	-	-	-	-	1	-	1	2	1	1	1	1	-	1	1	1	-	-	3
Glenforres	1	1	1	1	1	1	2	1	1	1	1	1	2	1	1	1	1	-	1	1	1	1	1	1	2
Glen Turret	3	1	3	1	1	2	2	1	1	3	2	-	2	-	1	1	-	3	-	1	2	1	-	1	3
Tullibardine	3	1	1	1	3	2	3	1	1	3	2	1	2	-	1	1	1	-	2	2	1	1	1	-	2

MALT SCOTCH WHISKY MAPS

for brands found in Whisky ... with Dinner

Scotland

Orkney

The
North
Sea

Lewis

Skye

Mull

Jura

The
Irish
Sea

England

General

Note: Due to the scale of the maps, locations of distilleries are only approximate. Some vatted brands are not shown.

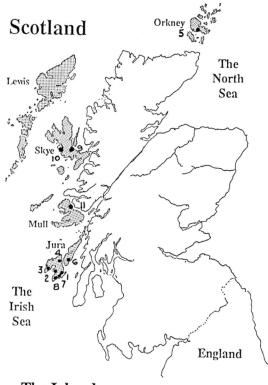

The Islands

Note: The brands listed in this compendium are only those to which reference is made in the book. There are many more, but they have not been "tested" - yet. There are also some that were on the market till only very recently but which have since ceased to exist and have become collector's items.

The following are traditional malt Scotch whiskies coming from the Islands:

1. Ardbeg
2. Bowmore
3. Bruichladdich
4. Bunnahabhain
5. Highland Park
6. Isle of Jura (Strathclyde)
7. Lagavulin
8. Laphroig
9. Poit Dhubh
10. Talisker
11. Tobermory

The next group that can be recognized as such with the minimum of dificulty is the Lowland group. Some malt Scotch whiskies in this group are traditionally listed in the Strathclyde region which embraces the old Campbeltown region with its two remaining brands, Glen Scotia and Springbank. It will be noted that the Central map combines both Perthshire and Stirlingshire. Wigtown and Ayr to the southwest are combined on another map.

12. Auchentoshan	}	17. Bladnoch	Wigtown
13. Glen Scotia	}	18. Deanston	Perthshire
14. Littlemill	} Strathclyde	19. Glengoyne	Stirlingshire
15. Springbank	}	20. Glenkinchie	E. Lothian
16. Ladyburn	Ayr	21. Rosebank	Stirlingshire

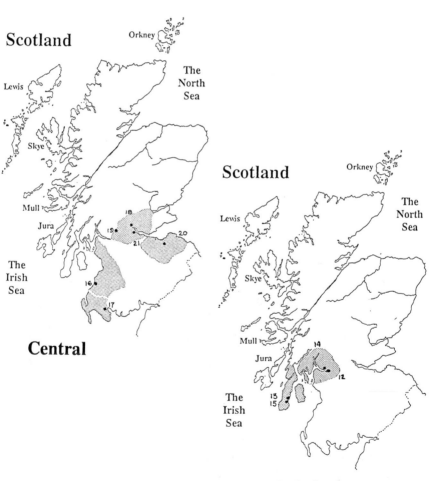

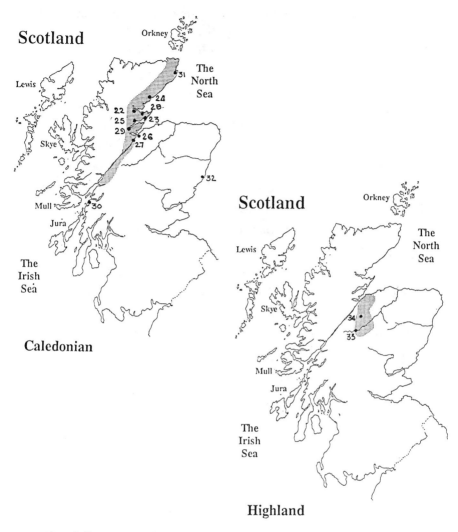

Scotland

Caledonian

Scotland

Highland

The following Caledonian malts are traditionally in the High-land category. We have redesignated them as Caledonian because of common taste characteristics and their location along the Caledonian Canal and up into the northern Highlands. They are slightly different than the true Highland malt.

22. Balblair

23. Ben Wyvis

24. Clynelish

31. Pulteney

Highland

25. Dalmore

26. Glen Albyn

27. Glen Mhor

32. Sheepdip

33. Dalwhinnie

28. Glenmorangie

29. Glenordie (Ord)

30. Oban (Strathclyde)

34. Tomatin

These malt Scotch whiskies comprise the major part of the Traditional Highland designation and are divided into their respective regions: Speyside (including Grampian), and Tayside.

Speyside

35. Aberlour
36. Auchriosk
37. Aultmore
38. Balvenie
39. Benriach
40. Benromach
41. Berry's Pure
42. Caperdonich
43. Cardhu
44. Craigellachie
45. Cragganmore
46. Dufftown
47. Fettercairn

48. Glenallachie
49. Glenburgie
50. Glendronach
51. Glendullan
52. Glen Elgin
53. Glenesk
54. Glenfarclas
55. Glenfiddich
56. Glengarioch
57. Glen Grant
58. Glenlivet (THE)
59. Glenmoray
60. Glenugie
61. Glenury-Royal

62. Inchgower
63. Knocando
64. Linkwood
65. Macallan
66. Milton Duff
67. Mortlach
68. Royal-Lochnagar
69. Strathconon
70. Strathisla
71 Tamdhu
72 Tamnavulin
73. Tomintoul

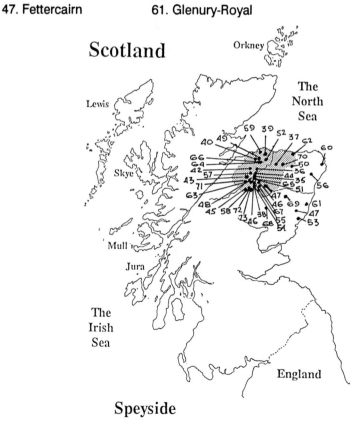

Speyside

Tayside

74. Blair Athol

75. Edradour

76. Glenforres

77 Glenturret

78. Tullibardine

Tayside

ANNEX A

An Quaich Official Tasting Form

The characteristics of the product(s) listed below are to be rated on a scale of 1 to 5 on the principle of least to most. The points are NOT to be totalled up. They are to serve as the basis of the summary in narrative form. The ratings and comments are merely the opinion of the taster and neither the taster nor An Quaich imply nor accept any legal or official responsibility whatsoever should this form be made public or used in any fashion whatsoever at any time without the express permission and under the conditions set down by both the taster and An Quaich. Expressions such as nutty, woody, earthy, wooly, oily and others are encouraged in order to give a better description of the product.

PRODUCT NUMBER	1	2	3	Summary

RATING:

VISUAL:
Colour (pale to dark)

Legs (surface tension -
    runny to heavy)

NOSE:
Attack (light to pronounced)

Presence (slight to strong)

Persistence (volatile to
    persistent)

TASTE:
Body (light to full)

Bite (delicate to definite)

Smoke (slight to heavy)*

Peat (slight to heavy)*

After-taste (fleeting to
    lingering)

Flavour (tasters description) 1_____ 2_____ 3_____

* Constitutes the "Balance"

PROBABLE 1. region_____ sub-region_____ brand_____
I.D.

    2. region_____ sub-region_____ brand_____

    3. region_____ sub-region_____ brand_____

ANNEX B

An Quaich

Whisky Nosing Test

Kindly Note:

DO NOT *taste* any of the samples
contained in the NOSING glasses.

CHECK FOR THE FOLLOWING:
1. Colour
2. Legs
3. Attack onthe nose
4. Persistence of smell
5. Presence (strength) of smell

 An Quaich

Whisky Nosing Test

Each whisky brand is identified by a lettered sticker.
The glasses with numbers contain the same whiskies
but in random order. The object is to match the
numbers with the letters.

Lagavulin	1	
Talisker	2	
Oban	3	
Cragganmore	4	
Dalwhinnie	5	
Glenkinchie	6	

Name:...

ANNEX C

an quaich malt Scotch whisky imports Canada Ltd.

RULES AND REGULATIONS

We, the undersigned, wishing to promote the knowledge and appreciation of malt Scotch whisky; to meet socially on a regular basis for the appreciation thereof; and to pool our resources for the placing of private stock orders, hereby proclaim the formation of a society to be known as An Quaich, signifying "drinking cup" for the purposes set out above and subject to the rules and regulations hereunder:

NAME AND NATURE

1. The group shall be known as a society bearing the name "An Quaich". The society is an association of individuals wishing to group together for the purposes set above.

2. The society is a non-profit and no officer thereof may gain financially by membership therein.

PRINCIPAL ADDRESS

3. As an incorporated body, there is no Head Office. The affairs of the society, however, shall be conducted from the City of......... under the name of the society and at the address of the Convenor.

MEMBERSHIP

4. Membership in the society shall be open to any interested person having attained the age of majority and who is not, by law or otherwise, knowingly precluded from consuming alcohol.

5. Membership shall not be limited to any set number unless members so decide by majority vote of the members present at the first Annual General meeting.

6. Membership may be terminated by the Convenor for non-payment of dues or other debts on the part of a member. Such member shall receive two (2) weeks notice in writing. Any member may resign at any time by so advising the Convenor on the condition that any dues or other debts have been paid and that no monies are due the society.

FEES

7. The fees shall be in the amount of $......per year per member. There is no fee for occasional escorts, other than the "cover charge." The fee for escorts participating on a regular basis shall be $......per year.

EXPENSES

8. Any out of the ordinary expense not anticipated in the budget shall be duly noted and reported to the membership at the next convenient meeting. Such expenses shall be prorated among the members and the society reimbursed accordingly.

OFFICERS

9. There shall be an officer designated as Convenor. The Convenor shall be responsible for all the administration of the society including banking and signing documents. The Convenor shall be responsible for convening all members to meetings and for providing an appropriate location.

10. The Convenor shall also be the agent for the society and shall supervise the administration of all private stock orders by members, in accordance with the procedures laid down by the Corporation.

11. The Convenor shall be elected at the Annual General Meeting of the society.

12. None of the above shall preclude the Convenor from acquiring any administrative assistance required or deemed necessary to function properly.

MEETINGS

13. There shall be a General Meeting to be held with one (1) week of the thirtieth (30) day of November of each and every year.

14. There shall not be less than four (4) meetings in any one year.

15. All meetings shall be convened by mail with at least two (2) weeks notice, and members are required to respond within one (1) week for organizational purposes.

16. Any member having signified intention of attending who does not do so shall remain liable for any costs incurred.

BOOKS

17. The finances of the society shall be recorded by the Convenor in a proper set of books which shall be subject to audit by any member or any other recognized authority at any time.

WINDING UP

18. If, through lack of interest, the society decides to wind up as an entity, all just debts shall be paid by the Convenor, to be reimbursed by the members at the last meeting on a prorated basis. If, on the other hand, there are funds remaining in any account after all just debts have been paid, any residue shall be forwarded to the Corporation.

AMENDMENTS

19. These rules and amendments may be amended at any time at a regular or Annual General Meeting by a two-thirds (2/3) majority vote of members present, subject to ratification by the Corporation.

THE CORPORATION

20. The "Corporation" is the parent body of all An Quaich chapters. It is incorporated under the Canada Corporations Act under the name "An Quaich Malt Scotch Whisky Imports Canada Ltd." with Head Office in the City of Ottawa.

21. Private Stock Orders from any and all members must be channelled through the Corporation in order to provide the benefits of bulk purchases.

22. Every Chapter shall remit to the Corporation each and every year, a sum equal to 20% of the membership dues collected but not less than a sum equal to $15.00 per regular member and $2.00 per regular escort.

23. Every Chapter shall benefit from any and all bulk discounts on all related material obtainable through the Corporation.

BIBLIOGRAPHY

BEROLZHEIMER, Ruth. Delineator Cook Book, Garden City Publishing Co. Inc., Garden City, New York, 1950.

BOUDART, Michel. Kinetics of chemical processes. Prentice-Hall, Englewood, N.J., 1968.

BRANDER, Michael. A Guide to Scotch Whisky, Johnston & Bacon Books Limited, Stirling, Scotland, 1975.

BRANDER, Michael. The Original Scotch, Clarkson N, Potter, Inc., Publisher, New York.

COOPER, Derek. The Century Companion to Whiskies, Century Publishing Company, London W1V 5PA, 1978, 1983

COOPER, Derek & PATTULLO, Dione. Enjoying Scotch, Cassell Ltd., Square, London, WC1R 45G. 1980.

DAICHES, David. Let's Collect Scotch Whisky, Jarrold & Sons Ltd., Norwich, 1986.

DEFAY, Raymond. Tension superficielle et adsorption, Liège, Editions Desoer, 1951

DI CORCIA, SAMPERI & SEVERNI, Gas Chromatographic column for the Rapit Determination of Congeners in Potable Spirits, Journal of Chromatography, 198 (1980) 347-353, Elsevier Scientific Publishing Company, Amsterdam.

EMERY & BREWSTER. The New Century Dictionary, Appleton - Century - Crofts inc., New York.

FORD, Gene. The Benefits of Moderate Drinking, Wine Appreciation Guild, San Francisco, CA 94108, 1988.

JACKSON, Michael. Malt Whisky Companion, McGraw-Hill Ryerson, 1989

HALL, T. Proctor. New methods of measuring surface tension of liquids, 1894, (ISBN 0665344384)

JONES, Iris Price. Celtic Cookery, Christopher Davies, Swansea.

LAMOND, J & TUCEK, R. The Malt File, The Benedict Books, London, 1988.

LOCKHART, Sir Robert Bruce. SCOTCH, The Whisky of Scotland in Fact and Story, Putnam, London, 1951.

MCBAIN, C.S. The Present of the Past, The Braes of Glenlivet, Scotch Malt Whisky, 1978

McDOWALL, R.J.S. The Whiskies of Scotland, Abelard-Schuman Limited, London, 1967.

MILLROY, Wallace. Malt Whisky Almanac, Lochar Publishing, Bankhead, 1987.

NATIONAL RESEARCH COUNCIL OF CANADA. In House Tests for Contents of Congeneric Elements in Potable Spirits, unpublished.

SIMPSON, TOON, GRANT, et al. Scotch Whisky, Macmillan Ltd., London, 1974.

SKIPWORTH, Mark. The Scotch Whisky Book, The Hamlyn Publishing Group Limited, Twickenham, Middlesex, 1987.

SOLOMONRAJ, G. The Gas Chromatographic Estimation of Ethanol, Acetaldehyde, and Acetone in Ethanol Metabolism Studies, Clinical Toxicology, 4(1), pp. 99-113, March 1971.

TOSHIBA OF CANADA LTD. Everyday Microwave Cooking for Everyday Cooks, Toshiba America Inc., Willowdale, Ontario 1979.

WALKER, Jearl. What causes the "tears" that form on the inside of a glass of wine? The Amateur Scientist.

WAUGH, William. The Whiskies of Scotland, John Murray Publishers, London, 1986.

About the Author

BERNARD EMILE POIRIER, a native Ottawan, was born into the military and raised in the shadows of Quebec City's historic Citadel. A graduate of the University of Ottawa in political science and law, he applied his love of logistics and research to the military, government, association administration, the Canadian Astronaut Program, and emergency preparedness.

Spare time during those forty-one years was devoted to the pursuit of fine arts, more academic degrees, teaching sailing and coastal piloting, and of course, very serious research into all aspects of malt Scotch whisky. The latter avocation led to a collection of over eighty brands, all personally tested, and to which additions are still being made.

He is a semi-retired "professional" volunteer with numerous asociations in the fields of acquatics and emergency preparedness, principally with the Canadian Red Cross Society.

He enjoys writing and has published numerous articles on legal matters related to his various occupations. He also loves good food and that, combined with his interests in malt Scotch whisky, inevitably led to this book. He and his wife Carmen are parents, grandparents, and living happily everafter.

Bernard Poirer (left) with Ian Bain at a tasting.